D1585969

Stories of
Solidarity

For my great-grandparents Samuel Francis (1852–1926)
and Elizabeth Francis (1853–1941)

for our son Samuel Prys Francis (1980–1997)

and for Mair, my lifelong comrade
born in the year of the NHS and founder of DOVE

Through their lives they taught me
about compassion and solidarity

Stories of
Solidarity

HYWEL
FRANCIS

First impression: 2018
© Hywel Francis & Y Lolfa Cyf., 2018

Cover design: Y Lolfa
Cover photograph: National Union of Mineworkers
(South Wales Area)

ISBN: 978-1-912631-03-2

Published and printed in Wales
on paper from well-maintained forests by
Y Lolfa Cyf., Talybont, Ceredigion SY24 5HE
e-mail ylolfa@ylolfa.com
website www.ylolfa.com
tel 01970 832 304
fax 832 782

In our hands is placed a power greater than their hoarded gold,
Greater than the might of armies magnified a thousandfold,
We can bring to birth a new world from the ashes of the old,
For the union makes us strong.

– Last verse of Ralph Chaplin's 'Solidarity Forever' (1915), anthem of the Industrial Workers of the World (the Wobblies).

In the struggle my sympathies were not neutral. But in telling the story of those great days I have tried to see events with the eye of a conscientious reporter, interested in setting down the truth.

– J. R., New York, 1 January 1919
Preface to John Reed, *Ten Days that Shook the World* (1961 edition), p.xiii.

… although the posts keep knocking out you had an embarrassment of help, and it really makes you realise what grand guys these people are, they just are the salt of the earth, no danger keeps them from an injured man … it's a sort of *esprit de corps* that you get underground … I've never met it anywhere in the world.

– Interview of Dr Dafydd Aubrey Thomas by Charles Parker about Onllwyn Colliery (1961).

As we walked through the double swing-doors [at Onllwyn Miners' Welfare] the level of the conversation dropped for a moment. Then someone started clapping and the rest followed. They were applauding us and all they knew about us was that we were queer and that we supported their cause unconditionally [in 1984].

– Mike Jackson, secretary of the Lesbian and Gays Support the Miners in Hywel Francis, *History On Our Side: Wales and the 1984–85 Miners' Strike* (2015), p.9.

Contents

Preface

WHAT TREMENDOUS HISTORY WE have here! Arguably it is only in South Wales that one can still get a sense of the wonderful socialist, communist and trade union traditions that have sadly, largely, disappeared in other parts of Britain.

Hywel Francis writes from real experience and a strong sense of commitment. Thanks to him we can feel the passions that swept through the valleys and the struggles that took place. He is a historian who brings it all to life, a politician who took part in epic events and a socialist who understood the position of the working class and what could be done to achieve real progress. He writes also about his family which had such a strong influence on his thinking.

Some of the events in this book may have been almost forgotten outside South Wales, others are still vivid as if they had just happened. And I learned so much that I hardly knew. It is an enthralling journey with special emphasis on the miners, and the key part that the South Wales Miners' Federation played in their lives. How many outside South Wales remember the Anthracite Miners' strike of 1925? We learn more about recent strikes under Thatcher, and the widespread support there was throughout the country. He describes the part played by the women of South Wales and also how the LGBT community came to the valleys to provide support.

Hywel writes also about the strong sense of internationalism among the miners. Many went to Spain to join the International Brigades and to fight for the republic against Franco in 1937/38. Later the local communities welcomed Basque refugees just, as more recently, they have hosted Syrian families. Hywel tells about visits to the valleys by Paul Robeson, how the miners supported Nelson Mandela and the struggle against apartheid.

Richard Burton, the Welsh Language Society, the chapels, rugby and poetry are all part of the rich South Wales tapestry. There is Josef Herman, a Pole who escaped the Nazis and lived for a time in Ystradgynlais and became a wonderful artist. It is ironic that the film of the Czech village of Lidice, *The Silent Village*, which was wiped out by the Nazis in 1942 was set in Ystradgynlais.

Aneurin Bevan was one of South Wales' most eminent politicians and his establishment of the NHS represented probably the greatest political achievement by any Government and this volume goes some way to explain how the special kind of solidarity within the South Wales valleys shaped the progressive ideas enshrined in the NHS.

Hywel himself played a part in much of this history. He was a hugely effective MP and I was privileged to be a member of the Joint Committee on Human Rights which he chaired. Among his many achievements he introduced the Carers Bill which became law in 2004 and improved the lot of carers.

I will end on a very personal note. As a Jewish child leaving Prague on the *Kindertransport* in 1939 I know something about solidarity and compassion. Against the odds people reach out and help. This is why I believe this book is about now and the future.

Lord Alf Dubs

Acknowledgements

THE PAPERS PRINTED HERE first appeared in the following works and are reprinted by kind permission of the original publishers. I also wish to acknowledge my thanks to family, friends, and colleagues for writings, lectures, speeches and funeral orations which have received their help, support and encouragement.

1 *The Times Higher Education Supplement*, 22 September 1995.
2 *Llafur*, Vol. 1, No. 2, 1973.
3 *A People and a Proletariat: Essays in the History of Wales 1780–1980* (ed. David Smith), Pluto Press, London, 1980. www.plutobooks.com.
4 Martin Jacques, then editor of *Marxism Today*, for inviting me to write the article published in February 1985.
5 Hywel Teifi Edwards (gol./ed.) *Cyfres y Cymoedd: Nedd a Dulais* (Gomer, 1994); *Llafur*, Vol. 6, No. 3, 1994.
6 Jeff Davies, chair of Seven Sisters RFC, for allowing me reprint two chapters from my *Magnificent Seven: The Centenary History of Seven Sisters Rugby Football Club* (Gwasg Morgannwg, 1997).
7 *The Welsh Journal of Education*, Vol. 6, No. 1, 1997.
8 The editor of *Cincinnati Post*, 6 June 1988.
9 The family of Will Lloyd for inviting me to give his funeral oration on 2 December 1986.
10 The family of Eirie Pugh for inviting me to give her funeral oration on 1 July 1993.
11 *History Workshop Journal*, Vol. 32, Issue 1, and Oxford University Press.

12   The family of Espe: Esperanza Careaga James for inviting me to give her funeral oration in December 2004.

13   Llyfrgell Genedlaethol Cymru/ National Library of Wales for reproducing the lecture on 12 July 2003, *The Bevan Foundation Review*, Issue 3, Winter 2003/04 and Daniel Williams (gol./ ed.) *Canu Caeth: Y Cymry a'r Affro-Americaniaid* (Gomer, 2010).

14   Llyfrgell Genedlaethol Cymru/ National Library of Wales for reproducing the lecture on 5 November 2005.

15   The Bevan Foundation for reproducing the lecture on 16 July 2005 and the subsequent pamphlet (2005).

16   The family of Richard Burton and Neath Port Talbot County Borough Council for inviting me to speak at the opening of the Richard Burton Trail, 10 June 2011.

17   Dr Victoria Winckler of the Bevan Foundation for inviting me to write the blog, 12 January 2012.

18   *Transactions of the Honourable Society of Cymmrodorion*, New Series, Vol. 18, 2012.

19   My friend David Carpanini for inviting me to give the lecture on 24 January 2014.

20   My former colleagues and friends in Parliament including members and staff of the Joint Committee on Human Rights, especially Lord Alf Dubs, Mike Hennessy and Murray Hunt in helping shape the ideas for the lecture on 10 March 2014.

21   My friends in Byw Nawr especially Baroness Ilora Finlay and Veronica Snow for advice on the lecture on 11 May 2017.

Footnotes have been removed throughout: the reader is directed to the original publications if requiring information on my sources.

I wish to thank Alun Burge, George Brinley Evans, Dai Havard, Deian Hopkin, Rob Humphreys, Daryl Leeworthy, Dai Smith and Wayne Thomas for comments, help and encouragement in shaping the collection. I am grateful too to Sian Williams, head of research collections at Swansea University, for her expert advice at all times and all the staff at the South Wales Miners' Library, particularly Jonathan Davies and Mandy Orford, for their practical assistance.

I owe particular thanks to all my friends and comrades within the local miners' support group (which has been recently revived) especially Kay and Phil Bowen, the late Hefina Headon and Christine Powell along with Francis Devine in Ireland and the late Mark Ashton and Mike Jackson of Lesbians and Gays Support the Miners: they all showed me the true meaning of solidarity.

To the staff at Y Lolfa I owe a great debt especially Robat and Lefi Gruffudd for putting their faith in this volume and to Rhidian Griffiths and Eirian Jones for assistance with editing.

I also wish to record my profoud thanks to two inspirational teachers of history: Malcolm Thomas at Whitchurch Grammar School who urged me 'i fynd i Abertawe' where I was taught by the late Emeritus Professor Ieuan Gwynedd Jones.

I am extremely grateful to my dear friend and comrade Lord Alf Dubs for his kind words in his Foreword: from his origins in Prague and flight from Nazi persecution to his own lifelong commitment to international solidarity especially the cause of child refugees has all been truly inspirational.

And finally, I thank Hannah, Dafydd and Sam, and most of all Mair: their lives are woven into the stories of solidarity told in these pages.

Hywel Francis
August 2018

Introduction

I ASKED THE POLICEMAN A question in the darkness as the cold rain ran down our faces. Did he think the strike-breaking miners would come to work that morning? He looked at me with an air of certainty and ill-disguised local pride. The day before, a community picket had expressed its collective will through silence as the strike-breakers left the pit. The policeman had never experienced anything like it. He said that once there was violence on a picket-line, as he had seen in many of the English coalfields throughout the strike, the police knew they would always win. What he saw that morning was different: he believed they would not return and he was right. What neither of us knew was that my friend Phil Bowen, the local strike leader, had secretly rung one of the strike-breakers the night before and offered a compassionate hand of friendship and solidarity.

So too in Treforgan, the other pit in our village. The sympathetic manager allowed me as the chair of the local support group into the pit-head baths to speak to the strike-breaker. I asked him what he needed. He told me he was homeless, his wife had left him and taken their children and he wanted somewhere to pray. He agreed to re-join the strike when I promised to find him somewhere to live, which was eventually achieved through our contacts with the local Catholic church. In the meantime, I asked my friend Ali Thomas to take him to London for a break. Ali promised to take him to the 'biggest and best church', St Paul's Cathedral.

And then again, these tactics of non-violent social action took the unusual form of a *cymanfa ganu* outside a strike-breaker's house in Penrhos. All these peaceful activities were often influenced and led by women and children, including my wife Mair and our children Hannah and Dafydd. Their outlook was reinforced by my mother, at home looking after our youngest, Sam. She would speak quietly to them of the earlier struggles of 1921, 1926, 1972 and 1974. But Mair, Hannah and Dafydd had their own immediate experiences. They and others in our valley had been influenced earlier in the year by their solidarity visits to the women's peace-camp at Greenham Common.

By contrast to all this, outside our support group area, in Ystalyfera, a poorly organised, verbally violent crowd intimidated and alienated an isolated strike-breaker who had been deceived back to work by older miners, some of whom we believed were there hiding anonymously in the crowd, doing most of the shouting and threatening to overturn a police-car. Solidarity comes in many forms: this was not one of them.

Another friend of mine, the Rev. John Morgans, was the leader of the Welsh Council of Churches who played a vital role in the Wales Congress in Support of Mining Communities which I chaired. He told me a revealing story at this time. He had discussions with South African church leaders who John believed had links with the banned African National Congress. They told him that calls for peace in our coalfields had to be accompanied by a struggle for justice.

John told me that he had a second conversion during that fateful strike of 1984–85. I believe I had a few secular 'light bulb' moments during that period too. Simultaneously, as a historian, adult educator and political activist, praxis took on a new meaning when solidarity and compassion were strained to new limits in our communities. They never truly recovered.

In 1859 my great-grandfather Samuel Francis was carried to work at the local colliery by his father who would claim an extra four trams while the child slept at the coalface. He was seven years of age and had been born in Pheasant Road in the mining village of Trebanos in the Swansea Valley.

Sam grew up to be a most 'valued' employee of the Dulais Valley coal-owner Evan Evans-Bevan. He was a farrier and 'vet' for all the owner's horses in the valley. When a horse was killed in an accident underground, my father would often tell me, another had to be bought. However, when a miner was killed there was little or no compensation. Sam appears not to have had any formal education. He was essentially an auto-didact and the proud owner of a substantial library of books on the care of horses.

Sam Frank, as he was known within the family and the community, and his wife Elizabeth (Betsie to the family) were to lose one son, Dafydd, in a colliery accident in 1908 and my father took his name and his place in their home. Sam was to die at the end of the 1926 miners' lockout and it seems that my father, living with his widowed grandmother, became the assumed head of the family as he entered the world of work as a collier-boy working alongside his father in Onllwyn No. 1 Colliery in December 1926.

Betsie was a formidable character in her own right: she helped to establish a small shop and billiard hall, raised five children and cared for, from time to time, three grandchildren including my father from the age of four. It was Sam and Betsie who brought the Francis family to Front Row, Onllwyn, in the Dulais Valley from 'ochr draw' – 'the other side'– as the Swansea Valley was described, and nearly one hundred and thirty years later we are still here.

By the time another Samuel Francis was born, our son in 1980, it was a very different world. He had Down's syndrome along with a serious heart condition. He died in 1997 having benefited from the care of the National Health Service and a bilingual state education. Mair, my wife and comrade of over fifty years and founder of the DOVE Workshop at Banwen in the Dulais Valley, was Sam's main carer supported by me, his siblings Hannah and Dafydd, and my late mother Catherine.

This collection is dedicated to these four family members in the Dulais Valley, spread over five generations, Sam and Betsie and Mair and Sam, who share a common story of compassion and solidarity.

I was born in Onllwyn in the Dulais Valley and the second annual carnival to celebrate the D-Day of 1944 halted outside our bungalow. Bob Robinson from Beacon's View called on my mother, through his loud-hailer, to show the new baby to the carnival. As a historian I have occasionally been told that my style has erred too often on the side of celebration, maybe subliminally influenced by that early experience. I hope with the passage of time I am at last trying to be more reflective in questioning some of this approach without losing too much of my passion. There was much nevertheless to celebrate and to be inspired by too. Fascism had been defeated, war had ended and there was a Labour Government already elected on what was a radical socialist programme. And the carnival had a practical purpose: to raise funds for a new Welfare Hall. This was to be achieved within a decade and became known from time to time as 'The Palace of Culture', a cause for celebration and pride given its celebrated role in the 1984–85 miners' strike; and in 2018 it was to be memorialised by a permanent photographic exhibition in the hall.

It has always been my view that we should never apologise for celebrating communities which place great store on solidarity. That act of celebration should define us. The late Professor Gwyn Alf Williams often described those who embraced our history as a means of understanding the present as 'people's remembrancers'. He said at the celebration meeting in 1981 for my father, a leader of the South Wales miners and a founder of the Wales TUC, that he was in that tradition. Gwyn had elaborated on this theme in his memorable 1978 *Merthyr Riots* BBC television history where he urged the Welsh to celebrate heroes not martyrs and become learners as well as teachers. That, in essence, is what this collection is about. It traces my journey as an apprentice historian, apprentice political activist and apprentice adult educator, through my essays, lectures, talks, speeches and funeral orations over the past five decades and places great value on people's own memories as an important historical source. But the collection is not an exercise in nostalgia, rather, by uncovering the past, I seek to address the vexed questions of populism, racism and xenophobia of today.

When my family arrived at Onllwyn it was a mainly Welsh-speaking community, emerging largely in the early decades of the twentieth century, which, perhaps unconsciously, prided itself on its diversity. My parents counted amongst their friends and family in the locality a rich variety of names: Beamish, Macho, Esteban, Pascoe, Regan, Carpanini, Zamorra, Mathoulin, Isaac, Preddy, Cawsey, Vale, Cook, Onions, Whitney, Miller, Gimlett, Mitchell and Biggar, some of whose descendants have worn more than the occasional Welsh rugby jersey.

In the 1940s and 1950s ours was even from this distance a confident and optimistic mining community in that immediate post-war world in the western anthracite part of the South Wales coalfield. It had been shaped by the benign ideas and stories of local and international solidarity which most recently had defeated Fascism. I listened to the heroic but also painful stories of loss and defeat, around the kitchen table, in the miners' welfare hall and in the political meetings and rallies I attended with my father. This included the annual highlight, the Miners' Gala in Cardiff where in 1955 I was once photographed asking Aneurin Bevan for his autograph. He personified more than any other our collective confidence and optimism and the true meaning of solidarity.

That may not have been a majority experience as I grew up in the very much minority culture of a Communist and Christian mining family. This was a culture which simultaneously celebrated Welsh International Brigaders like Jim Strangward from Onllwyn who had died serving in the International Brigades, rugby players of both codes Billy Boston and Lewis Jones, the Christian missionary to China Dr Griffith John who as a boy had worked at Onllwyn colliery, the Welsh revolutionary poet Niclas Y Glais, the English actress Sybil Thorndike, the Irish playwright George Bernard Shaw and most important of all, black American singer and internationalist, Paul Robeson.

As a child I heard poignant and very personal family stories, and the most telling related to my own given names David or Dafydd and Hywel. My father was named Dafydd after his uncle who was killed in the local colliery, Cwm-mawr, aged twenty-six in 1908. According to story-telling within our family, my father was given the name by his mother as he was the first grandson to be born after the tragedy. But the Registrar anglicised his name, as was often then the case. My father never spoke to us of this but the strict all-Welsh rule within our home gave more than a clue as to what he thought of it.

And as if to honour his mother and his Christian Socialist upbringing in the chapel and in the home, he always said that among his favourite Welsh hymns was 'Arwelfa'. When asked by a seemingly erudite BBC interviewer why would a communist and miners' union leader have such a strange hinterland, he said it was because it was his mother's favourite and was he not aware of the first two lines of the second verse? The nonplussed broadcaster, revealing a rather one-dimensional understanding of Wales and its people, was reminded of the real meaning of the words:

O mor hoff yw cwmni'r brodyr
Sydd â'u hwyneb tua'r wlad

[O how fine it is to have the company of brothers,
With their face towards the land.]

But the way my father explained it in Welsh, with the seeming authority of both a Sunday school-teacher and a Marxist workers' education tutor, it was more about having the strength of the solidarity of comrades, when confronted by the greatest of adversities.

My other given name came from my uncle Hywel who died of shock, aged only four, when he fell, whilst playing in front of the fire, into a bath of scalding hot water which was awaiting his uncle's return from work at the local colliery.

The searing experience of personal loss was indeed eased by collective religious and social solidarity which at different times and place could also be described as fellowship, as neighbourliness, as comradeship, as caring and as compassion. But that was done through the building of social institutions of all kinds, initially churches and chapels, then friendly societies and cooperative societies, institutes and welfare halls, sporting and cultural organisations, political bodies and trades unions, most notably the South Wales Miners' Federation, the Fed.

This collection seeks then to explore the experience of solidarity. Some of the essays are previously unpublished, others are long out of print. Implicitly and explicitly, they mirror my life as a historian, an adult educator and a political activist: these roles often overlapped, even converged, as in the 1984–85 miners' strike. I have never felt conflicted by this. Indeed I have always felt it a natural way of living, working and writing.

The common theme is the importance of the received collective memory in sustaining a sense of solidarity, both locally and internationally. Much of my work, as a historian and in politics, has been about listening to people's stories, their memories, their fears, their hopes and their aspirations, and then in turn, to speak and to write about them, shaped by the cultural and political influences of my parents' generation and my own generation.

I have decided to publish this collection now for two reasons. Firstly, with the seventieth anniversary of the founding of the National Health Service in July 2018, I felt we needed to be reminded of the ideological and community rootedness of the NHS in our mining communities, notably but not exclusively, Tredegar. My own father in our community of Onllwyn played a proud if modest part in this social and political achievement. Most significantly, we need to understand that the NHS was the single most important piece of legislative social solidarity of the twentieth century not just in Britain but across the world. As Aneurin Bevan, the Secretary of State for Health and Housing, said in introducing the National Health Service Bill in 1946, it would 'lift the shadow from millions of homes' and that 'The essence of a satisfactory health service is that rich and poor are treated alike, that poverty is not a disability, that wealth is not an advantage'.

We need to understand properly and fully that the NHS was the culmination of many acts of solidarity over many decades and can be explained by the words, actions and memories of men and women working together, particularly across the South Wales Valleys.

It should also be remembered that 2018 is the one hundred and twentieth anniversary of the founding of the South Wales Miners' Federation and, whilst there are virtually no working miners left in South Wales, its benign influence endures through the NHS and through the Bevan Foundation whose journal places great store on recognising 'resilient communities' which still value social solidarity.

Secondly, as the coalfield disappears and the communities which grew out of it fracture under the added weight of UK Government austerity policies, so also does the collective memory.

Communities which had built unity from a diversity of peoples and often in the most challenging times of depression and war, created a progressive, cosmopolitan, caring and internationalist vision which gave birth to the NHS.

And now threatening that, fuelled by globalisation and neo-liberal austerity policies, there appears to be a growing collective amnesia, an introspection, a corrosive parochialist, almost nativist anti-immigrant 'victim' culture in communities with no immigrants to speak of but which only a handful of generations ago were shaped by immigrants from Bilbao to Bethesda and Bardi.

A decade or so ago I listened to the people of Blaenau Gwent speak persistently and depressingly of their problems being caused by immigrants. I wrote of it at the time in the *Western Mail* (15 August 2006):

> Candidates in the recent Blaenau Gwent by-election faced one question with particular regularity. 'Are you local?' Such a question would not have been posed to Alan Sapper, the trade union leader, when he arrived as a war-time evacuee in Tonypandy. Alan said to me in 1971 when I worked at the TUC, 'Tonypandy had a fine internationalist and anti-fascist spirit ...' There are those of us who still believe that the Valleys will always be defined by the welcoming of so-called foreigners, whether they were Basque refugees, Italians to Cwm, evacuee children from the East End, or Paul Robeson to Ebbw Vale in 1958.

Ideas of solidarity are today, as ever, contested territory even if the challenges seem more daunting in seeking to achieve a cultural hegemony. I am very conscious that there appears, for the moment, to be a 'collective amnesia' relating to our recent past which can potentially turn out to be very dangerous. In opening up a public debate on all this we should be cautious about condemning those who do not embrace our 'progressive' view of the world, assuming that we not only speak for them but also too often at them. That may be one of the lessons of the 2016 Referendum.

That said, we should indeed celebrate and cherish those 'resilient' places where the flame still burns brightly. There are former mining communities squeezed by global forces which are still able to develop localised strategies based on the universal values of education, social justice and social solidarity, as with the Dulais Valley's DOVE Women's Training Workshop and Ystradgynlais' Friends and Neighbours group which welcomes Syrian refugees to their midst. Such initiatives play their part in sustaining proudly the benign collective memory of solidarity.

One historian has recently put the challenge very succinctly: 'Our urgent question is how we can escape our present confusion and reconnect with historical reality in a way that is tragically denied to sufferers of dementia, finding a new global role as cultures that embrace the realities of their long and complex pasts and refashion their heritage for the common good.' (David Andress, *Cultural Dementia: How the West has lost its History, and Risks Losing Everything Else*, 2018, p.6.)

This volume falls naturally into three collections. Firstly, working on the premise that our understanding of solidarity and human rights begins with our immediate local experiences, I have used Eleanor Roosevelt's vivid descriptor, 'Where, after all, do universal human rights begin? In small places, *close to home…*' ('The Great Question', address at the UN in New York in 1958.)

This first collection maps out the community and family roots which have shaped my approach by highlighting the history of my village, my valley, my rugby team and my particular academic work at my university.

I begin with a short essay entitled 'Making the Road by Talking', which brings together the various strands of solidarity explored throughout the volume: the local and the international perspectives; story-telling, pathos and humour; education, culture and politics. A version of it appeared on 22 September 1995 in *The Times Higher Education Supplement*. I valued then as I do now oral history as a legitimate form of research and scholarship, recognising as it does the authentic voice of those who have made history but who have for the most part until recent times been written out of history.

The next seven contributions, written between 1973 and 1997, illustrate the inter-relationship between received collective memory, popular culture, education and solidarity.

My essay about the Anthracite Strike of 1925, published in *Llafur* in 1973, tells of a localised strike which my father witnessed as a boy: marching gangs of striking miners led by their brass bands were building solidarity across the anthracite coalfield against the victimisation of union activists. I undertook research into this strike because of the received collective memory within my community, transmitted to me as a child and again as a young researcher by my father and his friends, notably Dai Dan Evans, Dick Beamish, Dick Cook and the one-time Labour MPs for Llanelli and Neath, James Griffiths and D. J. Williams respectively. This research was part of a much wider exercise I had initiated in 1971 at University College Swansea, a three-year rescue operation funded by the Social Sciences Research Council which created the South Wales Miners' Library and South Wales Coalfield Archive.

The essay 'The Secret World of the South Wales Miner: The Relevance of Oral History' was first published in 1980 in David Smith's *A People and a Proletariat*. It is based on over a decade of oral history work centring on three major themes: firstly, my doctoral thesis on Welshmen who fought in the Spanish Civil War, 'The South Wales Miners and the Spanish Civil War: a Study in Internationalism' (1978), later published as *Miners against Fascism: Wales and the Spanish Civil War* (1984); secondly, a trade union and social history of the coalfield, written with Dai Smith, *The Fed: a History of the South Wales Miners in the Twentieth Century* (1980); and finally research into what ultimately became a lifelong obsession, the role of workmen's institute libraries, which I had written about initially in *The History Workshop Journal* in 1976 in my essay 'The Origins of the South Wales Miners' Library' and more recently with Sian Williams in our *Do Miners Read Dickens? Origins and Progress of the South Wales Miners' Library, 1973–2013* (2013).

That 1980 essay explores through oral testimony the personal, often difficult to capture, experiences of the peoples of the South Wales coalfield in the early decades of the twentieth century: the experiences of immigrants, of child labour, of women in domestic service, of opposition to war. It makes salutary reading for the Valleys of today. My approach benefited enormously in the 1970s from working with the two great pioneers of oral history, George Ewart Evans and Charles Parker, and also with members of the adult education history classes I organised in the Neath, Dulais, Swansea and Aman valleys.

The two central essays in this section are deeply personal. The first, 'My Community, My Valley: Onllwyn, Cwm Dulais' was originally written in Welsh for my friend and adult education colleague Hywel Teifi Edwards in his series *Cyfres y Cymoedd: Nedd a Dulais* (1994) at the time of the National Eisteddfod, and subsequently appeared in *Llafur* (1994) in English. The second, 'My Club: "Magnificent Seven"' derives from my history of Dulais Valley's Seven Sisters RFC (1997) of which I am proud to be President.

This section ends with the essence of my inaugural professorial lecture at University College Swansea in 1994 which outlines the personal and intellectual ideas underpinning my work as an academic in building stronger relationships between communities and their universities. The lecture here entitled 'Communities,

Universities and a New Beginning' explains how the South Wales Miners' Library and the Community University of the Valleys came into being in 1973 and 1993 respectively 'close to home'.

At the centre of this first section is a very political article, 'Mining the Popular Front', written in the heat of battle, full of optimism when I was chair of the Neath, Dulais and Swansea Valleys Miners' Support Group and the Wales Congress in Support of Mining Communities. It is a creature of its time, highly polemical and full of emotion. It is one of several I wrote for *Marxism Today* in the mid 1980s. In many respects the lessons I learnt in 1984–85 were put to good effect when I became head of a besieged Department of Extra-Mural Studies at University College Swansea: wars of position, hegemony and historic compromise were lessons revisited in the calmer world of the campus.

The second group of writings, entitled 'Things International', is inspired by Jim Brewer, secretary of the International Brigades Association (Cymru) whose speech at the fiftieth anniversary in Ystrad Rhondda in 1986 of the outbreak of the Spanish Civil War and the launch of the Wales-Nicaragua Solidarity Movement, referred to the South Wales Miners' Federation (the Fed) as 'our link with things International'. I explore in several of my contributions the personal and family traumas of the Spanish anti-fascist struggle. They reveal aspects of solidarity invariably overlooked, yet which can often be the most profound.

I begin with what turned out to be a hopelessly optimistic newspaper article for the (now defunct) *Cincinnati Post* (6 June 1988), which focuses on an enduring preoccupation and fascination for me, the links between the Appalachian coalfields of the US and our own South Wales coalfield. That relationship has taken on a new form with Tom Hansell's film *After Coal* (2016). I then explore the personal and political dimensions of Welsh solidarity in the 1930s with the Spanish anti-fascist cause, including three funeral orations. This section ends with two lectures I gave at the National Library of Wales. Firstly in 2003 to the Friends of the National Library of Wales I spoke on the special relationship between Paul Robeson and Wales, especially its miners. This was previously published in Welsh in Daniel G. Williams (gol./ed.), *Canu Caeth: Y Cymry a'r Affro-Americaniaid* (2010). Secondly in 2010 in giving the Annual Welsh Political Archive Lecture I outlined the connectedness of local and global struggles.

The final group of writings is called 'Bread and Roses!', which was the title of the 1911 poem by James Oppenheim whose final line, 'But a sharing of life's glories: Bread and roses! Bread and roses!' is particularly apposite. It is a reminder that the labour and trades union movement has a broad, indeed holistic, mission and vision. When the painter David Carpanini gave the 2017 Richard Burton Annual Lecture at Swansea University he praised the Port Talbot-born leader of the ASTMS union, Clive Jenkins, for his desire to introduce his members to a wide range of cultural influences. In the audience was my friend and one-time parliamentary colleague Dai Havard, who had worked as a senior lay official with Clive Jenkins. He felt that the inspirational lecture correctly challenged the notion that trades unions were just 'thugs' and 'barbarians' and 'no longer interested in educationally literate and rounded individuals'.

In that spirit of a more comprehensive definition of solidarity, these last writings mirror many of my lifelong concerns around the inter-relationships between memory, culture, education and caring, summed up in the notion of the personal is the political. They coincide with my time in Westminster as the Labour Member of Parliament for Aberavon from 2001 to 2015, specifically in relation to my Private Members' Bill, which became the Carers (Equal Opportunities) Act (2004), my work as chair of the Joint Committee on Human Rights (2010–15) and finally as chair of

Byw Nawr/Live Now, the end of life care coalition in Wales. In all of this work there emerges a definition of solidarity that is not narrow but inclusive and enabling, one that embraces ideas of fellowship, cooperation and compassion, 'close to home'.

Latterly, it has been my desire to celebrate the cultural achievements of our mining communities through Richard Burton, David Carpanini and Josef Herman, whose origins and lives exemplified the true meaning of compassion and solidarity. I have always felt that in defining culture in its broadest popular sense, artists, as Paul Robeson always said, have a vital role to play. That is why I have included my lecture to the Cymmrodorion in 2012 on 'London and the Miners' Strikes of the Twentieth Century', because the miners of South Wales have a story to tell about their own defnition of cultural solidarity.

This is explained most lucidly by Michael D. Higgins, now President of Ireland, when he talked of Raymond Williams' commitment to a politics that opposed economic exploitation, cultural domination and personal repression: hence the Gays and Lesbians Support the Miners loved the South Wales Striking Miners' Choir singing 'Comrades' to them. Until that time, where else had that happened in an industrial struggle? And what other trades union saw as its role the need to organise an annual cultural festival, the South Wales Miners' Eisteddfod? That is why, as my father deftly implied, the good Lord ensured that the sun always shone for the Miners' Eisteddfod, because the NUM organised it.

This collection seeks to ask the questions, 'have we lost that world?' and 'can we, in the words of that hymn of the Wobblies, "bring to birth a new world from the ashes of the old"?'.

I trust that this collection is an affirmation of that hope. The Canadian labour historian, David Frank, wrote in 1976:

> … it is never safe to assume that any of our history is altogether

dead. It tends to accumulate as a form of 'stored cultural energy' and from time to time moments of cultural transmission take place.*

Let us hope that we will live in that moment.

---

* David Frank, 'Class Conflict in the Coal Industry, Cape Breton, 1922' in Gregory S. Kealey, Peter Warrian (eds), *Essays in Canadian Working Class History* (1976) pp.183–184.

I

Close to Home

1

Making the
Road by Talking*

THERE WAS A TENSE inquest at the Blaenllechau Radical Club. The committee was discussing the theft of the new colour television. One member provided his explanation: 'you put it in a place where everyone could see it.'

The layers of meaning seem to increase over time. But this Valleys humour was lost in the translation, across the Atlantic back in 1979. Ivor England, humorist, raconteur, sage and miner from 'radical' Mardy – 'Little Moscow' – told the story to Barbara Angle, the miner novelist, and Myles Horton, founder of Highlander, that remarkable radical adult education centre in Tennessee. Barbara and Myles listened, at least for the moment, with polite incomprehension.

The life and times of the late Myles Horton were celebrated in a published conversation between himself and Paulo Freire entitled *You Make the Road by Walking* (1990). The book could easily have been entitled 'You Make the Road by Talking'. The disappearing art of 'storytelling' – could we even call them parables? – reminds us of the universal worth of a collectivist culture, whether rural or urban. I listened, not quite as an eavesdropping academic, to the transatlantic conversations of

---

* First published in *The Times Higher Educational Supplement*, 22 September 1995.

miners, women and men in the 1970s and 1980s. Some dreams but mostly fears for the future, often told through fictive stories. These are now invariably faint and haunting voices as the benign coalfield communities are destroyed and dispersed.

In recent times oral historians have 'legitimised' and rightly elevated the importance of storytelling so that reflective learning is truly recognised. I wonder however what a future Raymond Williams in a 'Towards 3000' would make of the current learning experiences of our own academic communities!

The book which has had the greatest impact on me is very much in this oral tradition. Chris Evans' *Industrial and Social History of Seven Sisters* (1964) was written by one of the true organic intellectuals of the Welsh working class. I read it before leaving for university and if ever there was a volume which legitimised my own life experiences and those of my community, then it was this one. Here is a sensitively written history of an industrial community in the western part of the South Wales coalfield in which this retired miner had shrewdly brought together the anecdotes of an oral tradition of over a century of social development. To some extent his closing paragraph predicts the demise of all coalfield communities today:

> Hirfynydd bears the scars of forestry, the young saplings have taken root, in a few years' time the surrounding mountains will once more be covered with that dark green look. Will the village then be forgotten? Will it return to the days of long ago with nothing to disturb its peaceful surroundings but the murmurings of the streams, the braying of the beasts and the sweet twittering of birds and the memories of old men?

I am now in that position of following the footsteps of the late Chris Evans in writing a specific history of Seven Sisters: the centenary of its rugby club, and much will depend on the way in which I collect and interpret those remarkable anecdotes from men and women. The biggest challenge will be satisfying my feminist partner. She will need to be convinced that I am on that journey from Valleys man to new man.

People like Chris Evans were the forerunners of what is now known as participatory research, working in coalition with social movements and the powerless, although the people of Seven Sisters would not see themselves as either powerless or disadvantaged.

I saw Ivor England again recently at the crowded funeral of the miners' leader Emlyn Williams. The air was thick with stories of our collective but disappearing past. I wanted Ivor to explain the real meaning of that particular story of the Blaenllechau Radical Club. Typical of the organic intellectual he is, the reply was 'which one of the stories do you mean?'

2

The Forgotten Strike of 1925 *

THE ANTHRACITE STRIKE IN 1925 can justifiably be seen as a forgotten strike, for outside the western part of the South Wales coalfield little or nothing is now remembered of those events that for a short while, in that long hot summer, gripped the imagination of the British Labour Movement and must have struck fear and horror in the hearts of all those bold shareholders who had sunk their capital in the new coal Combines of West Wales, that seemingly remote and hazardous part of the British Empire. The historian can only surmise as to the extent of their bewilderment not only by such a peculiar phenomenon as a 'Seniority Rule' ('Y Rheol Blaenoriaeth') but by such Edward Lear sounding villages as Seven Sisters, Tumble and Cross Hands and collieries bearing the unlikely nicknames 'Candy' (International), 'Clink' (Cwmllynfell) and 'Next Week' (Ystalyfera). Yet, although it was overshadowed and overtaken by the national events involving 'Red Friday' in July 1925, and, more significantly, the General Strike and Lockout of 1926, this localised struggle by thirty thousand anthracite miners was a landmark of immeasurable significance in the development of a

---

* First published as 'The Anthracite Strike and Disturbances of 1925' in *Llafur*, Vol. 1, No. 2, 1973.

sophisticated trade union consciousness among the whole of the South Wales miners.

The strike and disturbances can be seen as an inevitable clash between the desire of miners to protect long established customs and the growing coal Combines wishing to maximise the profitability of their concerns. This contradiction is thrown into sharp relief by the bald utterances of Dai Dan Evans, a miner at the International Colliery, Abercraf, and Frederick Alexander Szarvasy, the chairman of the United Anthracite Collieries:

> The difference between the leader and the ordinary rank and file in the anthracite area is much less than in the steam coal … In the anthracite area, if you wanted to dismiss a man who was a bit of a 'troublemaker', they would have to take possibly a hundred men out before him [because of the Seniority Rule] … [Consequently] you see you had lambs roaring like lions in the anthracite, and they had to be a lion to bloody well roar like a lion in the steam coalfield. (D. D. Evans).

> Regarding this Colliery [Ammanford No. 1] it seemed evident at the time the present Board took control that the working conditions had to be rearranged before satisfactory profits could be earned. (F. A. Szarvasy).

This dichotomy of interest was essentially a phenomenon which became more apparent in the early 1920s with the development of the coal Combines. The anthracite coalfield had been dominated by drifts and small levels owned largely by local farmers or 'self-improved' miners, supported by a mining engineer, a foreman and occasionally by additional capital from 'leading' members of the village. The mines were sufficiently small for recruitment to be limited to the immediate locality and consequently were very much village enterprises. The owner was known intimately by his employees as he had probably attended the same elementary school, Sunday school and continued to frequent the same chapel. Although there were often grievances, the pit, like the chapel and the public house, was part of a shared community experience of individual anthracite villages, and such grievances could be more easily resolved within such a context. Discontent with economic hardships and conditions must have been appreciated by the owner to the extent that he respected the miners' customs and did not normally challenge them. Similarly, the owner was content to receive a relatively moderate and leisurely return on his money and not answerable to a large and alien body of directors and shareholders demanding ever increasing returns.

The custom of the 'Seniority Rule', which became Rule 26 of the Anthracite District standing orders, grew out of such an enclosed society. When the coal trade temporarily fell away in the summer months, miners were allowed to migrate to the adjoining steam coalfield and return later to claim their old work places. Similarly, a miner could not be laid off at the discretion of the manager: he was protected by his date of employment and those most recently employed would be the first to be made redundant. Such a custom only existed in a universal sense in the Anthracite District of the South Wales Miners' Federation (SWMF) and has persisted in a modified way to the present day.

Ammanford, the focal point of the strike, was still very much a frontier town in the 1920s. It had many of the qualities of the Merthyr of the early nineteenth century. Convictions for drunkenness against young men in the town rose by 100 per cent in 1924. It was above all an industrial island in a rural sea. Anthracite mining in the area had not expanded a great deal until the early part of the twentieth century so that the bulk of the population was relatively young and mobile. Of its early trade union leaders, S. O. Davies and his brother Gibbon were from Aberdare, Evan (Ianto) Evans was a native of Tredegar, while Tom Williams was from Dafen, near Llanelli, and Edgar Lewis was born in the Rhondda. Jim Griffiths, from Betws, was probably the only locally-born leader.

The strike and disturbances can be traced directly to the economic development of capitalist coal Combines: a rationalisation and centralisation of ownership and control. By 1920, about three fifths of the output of the South Wales coalfield was under the control of four groups of allied interests. The Combines, however, came late to the Anthracite. But when the development materialised, it was all the more rapid and controversial, so that the pace must have contributed to the conflict. The Amalgamated Anthracite and the United Anthracite, both formed in 1924, became the two dominant Combines. Before the Combines swallowed the smaller colliery companies, anthracite miners 'enjoyed good conditions, good price lists and allowances and general customs. The control of these concerns was practically in the hands of the lodge committee'. The Combines seemed intent on eliminating the old customs so as to maximise the profitability of their new concerns.

The basic custom was the 'stint' whereby the miners controlled the maximum output of each workplace and in so doing provided the economic basis of their good conditions. The tactic of the Combines was to deliberately overcrowd each pit, especially with miners ignorant of local customs, fleeing 'from the spectre of unemployment to the harbour of continuous work'. In one of the many editorials urging greater militancy, the *Llanelli Labour News* outlined the essence of the strike:

> If the men will but preserve their customs, they can withstand the Trusts: once they lose their customs, the Trusts will do what they have done in the Rhondda.

With these economic developments in the early 1920s, the human contact between owner and miner was severed. A working anthracite miner of the period, D. J. Williams of

Gwaun-Cae-Gurwen (who later became the Labour MP for Neath, 1945–64) wrote lucidly of the situation:

> The growth of these powerful Combines effects a complete revolution in the relations of capital and labour in the coal industry. Time was when the colliery worker knew his employer personally. In those days, it was the custom of the owner himself to come round the faces to consider allowances, prices, special job rates, and to meet in person the workers and their representatives. Such is not the case now. The old relations of persons have given way to the new relation of things. The Combine is a vast machine, and the worker is merely a cog in it. He does not know his employers; probably he has never seen them. But the struggle between labour and capital still goes on, only it is now fought in a more intensive form. It is now a struggle between workers – through their organisation – and the vast unit known as the Capitalist Combine.

Immediately the United Anthracite took over the Ammanford No. 1 Colliery, where the 1925 strike began, a new manager was appointed and there began a series of intermittent struggles over such questions as the Combines attempt to eliminate a New Year's Day holiday, Good Friday holiday, the short Saturday shift and housecoal for lodgers as well as getting miners rather than firemen to carry powder. Many such customs were lost because there had been no previous written agreement.

On several occasions the lodge committee entered the pay office and refused to leave until the deficiencies were made up. The most critical attack came when, as a result of a change in the method of working in eight places in the Boxer District, the men fell back on minimum wage rates because the piece rates were considered inadequate. The colliery agent gave 116 miners notice to terminate their contracts and refused to recognise the matter as a dispute. The lodge offered a list of seniority but the management insisted on the same 116 becoming redundant, many of whom had completed twenty years' service. The Combine was thus attempting to sidestep the Seniority Rule and eliminate a traditionally militant district of the colliery.

The seemingly trivial occurrence which triggered off the actual strike came at the end of April with an open attack on the custom of two men in a place. The custom in Ammanford No. 1 Colliery was that a father could have his son to work with him so long as his regular partner would agree to work in another place, but such an arrangement would have to be sanctioned by a general meeting of the workmen. The management, however, failed to go through such a procedure when they attempted to move Will Wilson to another place. For this reason he refused to move and consequently was dismissed. The general meeting later the same day accepted the change, thus satisfying Wilson's sole objection. He turned up for work the following day but was not reinstated. The Federation Lodge claimed that Wilson was simply being loyal to a long-standing practice at the colliery. Yet the dispute apparently had its roots in an old quarrel between Will Wilson and the manager who was paying back 'an old score by depriving him of his livelihood'.

This dismissal of Wilson, and the bypassing of the General Meeting along with the closure of the militant Boxer District, was seen as a deliberate attack on the Seniority Rule, the most important of all customs in the anthracite, as it was clearly a fundamental safeguard against victimisation.

When the five local pits struck in sympathy with the victimised miners, the situation was beginning to spiral, according to Ianto Evans, one of the leaders of the newly formed strike committee. By 30 June, the *Western Mail*, mouthpiece of the coal-owners, gloomily reported that the whole of the Anthracite District was about to come out on strike, after the expiration of the fourteen days notices. It was widely believed that an attack on the Seniority

Rule in Ammanford could quite easily lead to a similar attack in all other parts of the Anthracite coalfield.

By 14 July, the second week of the strike, all miners were out except for some in the Dulais Valley and Vale of Neath. Their persistence in working was the occasion for two violent demonstrations. The scene is described by Ianto Evans:

> A mass meeting was arranged ... at the Glanaman Football Ground, and it was a glorious sight, thousands of workers being present, and by this time news had come through that these two collieries were working. Eventually a letter from a contact in the Dulais Valley was handed up to the chairman, Comrade Arthur Thomas, with the information regarding the position ... a resolution [was moved] that a demonstration proceeded that night to meet these workmen going to work the following morning ... The resolution was carried unanimously and a rush was made to Ammanford to get a crowd together, as no prior arrangements had been made. That night about four hundred strikers ... left Ammanford led by the Ammanford Band, and proceeded up the valley where they picked up the Cwmaman section, headed by their band, then to Gwaun-Cae-Gurwen and Brynaman, with another band each. Through the Swansea Valley the crowd gathered like a snowball and by the time the procession reached Ystradgynlais Common it was from 15,000 to 20,000 strong. They continued to march through the night until they got to Creunant in the Dulais Valley, 21 miles from Ammanford.

A skirmish occurred when the Ammanford pickets met the workmen's trains from Neath at Creunant station. The trouble apparently began only when knives were drawn by those miners wishing to go to work. This was sufficient to arouse the pickets who hauled the 'foreigners' (as the Neath men were considered to be) onto the platform and gave them 'cwpl o bunts'. They did not work for the remainder of the strike and were compelled to walk the six miles back to Neath. The police made an appearance at the station but were many times outnumbered and were 'a sight for the gods'. About twenty had arrived, quaking in their boots, absolutely cringing and begging the crowd to go away. After some windows were smashed at the house of Daniel Daniels, a director of the United Anthracite Combine, and further scuffles at Brynteg Colliery (Seven Sisters) as well as some momentous open-air meetings, the whole of the Dulais Valley miners joined the strike.

But the following day there was one pit left in the Anthracite District still working – the Rock Colliery at Glyn-neath. The events of that day became something of a local legend as 'The Battle of the Rock'. The Dulais Valley miners joined the thousands from the Amman and Swansea Valleys in marching over the Hirfynydd mountain to picket the Rock Colliery miners. They were led by a brass band and a police sergeant from Seven Sisters. Never had the mining communities of the Dulais Valley seen such crowds as this marching mass of miners which overwhelmed the valley; in the excitement, children absconded from school and followed the band. But the police had reacted quickly after the Creunant debacle and the miners, according to one participant, were marching 'into the jaws of the lion … In the early hours of the morning when the sun was rising, it was a lovely day by then, we could see in the distance the reflection of the sun on the helmets of the police that were up there'. The police allowed some of the marchers through their cordon, only to find a hundred-strong reserve force hiding behind a ditch. A police whistle blew and 'for ten minutes all you could hear was the clash of batons on the skulls of miners'. One miner, a veteran of the Great War, sounded 'the charge' on his bugle, only to add further confusion to the situation. This musical interlude does not seem to have been part of a carefully laid conspiracy. On the contrary, the whole affair was characterised by a total lack of 'strategic leadership'.

There were sixteen casualties, including Police Constable Bryn Phillips of Port Talbot, a boxer and international rugby forward, who was badly mauled. One young miner from Cwmtwrch, the sole supporter of a widowed mother and eight children, was so badly beaten by batonning about the head that he spent a long period in hospital and never worked as a miner again. The policeman responsible was not forgotten. The next occasion he played rugby against one of the Swansea Valley teams he received such leg injuries that he suffered permanent incapacity. Such was the hatred for those who attempted to undermine the strike. The effect of the disturbance was that the Rock Colliery miners joined the strike.

These two occurrences at Glyn-neath and Creunant were mere skirmishes compared with what was to follow. With the strike embracing all the anthracite miners, one of the strike leaders could claim that 'the rank and file were thoroughly aroused and were definitely forcing the pace and demanding a tightening up of the struggle, and the withdrawal of the safety men'. The safety men were compelled to call a special district meeting and by an overwhelming majority declared in favour of strike action: a unique and unprecedented decision in the whole history of the South Wales coalfield. But some officials persisted in working. The attempt by the coal-owners to save their pits by using 'volunteer' pumpsmen and to introduce extra police from other counties to protect their property and their 'blacklegs' only accelerated the trend towards violence.

July 28 saw the beginning of serious disorder and violence. From this moment onwards until 6 August, the town of Ammanford and some surrounding villages were under the virtual control of the Combine strike committee. On 28 July, there was trouble simultaneously at five collieries. The *South Wales Daily Post* reported that Gelliceidrim Colliery was rushed by a crowd of miners, some with hoods to hide their faces: 'mob law prevailed for a time', claimed the reporter. At Saron Colliery, officials were attacked, shots were fired, a man in the colliery yard was hit by a bullet and a quantity of explosives was discharged. Similarly, at Park Colliery, explosives were discharged and telephone wires were cut. There was also a large demonstration at the Emlyn Colliery, Penygroes, as well as at Cross Hands, where a crowd led by Edgar Lewis, the local check-weigher, 'terrified' the police by singing Doctor Joseph Parry's hymn-tune 'Aberystwyth'.

Extra police were brought into the area but seemed totally inadequate. Massive reinforcements were needed to try to break the strike. The *South Wales Daily Post* demanded: 'Extra police protection will probably be needed for the men to remain at work.' As a consequence, the Anthracite coal-owners appealed to the Chief Constables of Carmarthen, Glamorgan and Brecon for help. The Combine strike committee, however, knew of such moves well in advance as there were unusual 'friends' inside the Ammanford police station.

Again, on Thursday, 30 July, there were riotous disorders simultaneously at Ammanford Square, Ammanford No. 2 Colliery where there was a baton charge, at Betws, and also at Wernos, Pantyffynnon and Llandybïe Collieries. Evan Llewellyn, aged fifty, who was later given a seventeen months' prison sentence, was one of many who apparently openly incited riotous behaviour: 'I don't care a **** if there are twenty police. I will stand in front of all their bullets. We want to stop everyone going to work. They are not going to work while we are starving. What are the police? If they obstruct you, fight them.'

But the so-called 'Battle of Ammanford' did not occur until Wednesday, 5 August. Ianto Evans recalled that 'crowds of workers lined the streets demanding that a march be made to the Ammanford No. 2 Colliery … where an electrician had sneaked in on the pillion of a motor cycle … The police were concealed inside the colliery premises ready and waiting. Nothing daunted the crowd, [they] marched up and demanded that this man be removed. The Deputy Chief Constable led a force of police to the attack and was promptly laid out. Then the fun started.'

Some two hundred Glamorgan police had been billeted at a Gwaun-Cae-Gurwen brewery and were rushed to the scene. But the strike committee had already been kept well informed. A motor cyclist had been dispatched to Bridgend to reconnoitre all police movements. The committee was well prepared when the Glamorgan and Cardiff 'Irish' police, some allegedly drunk, travelled unsuspectingly in twelve buses along the Neath-Ammanford road. At Pontamman, there was an embankment on each side of the road, a perfect position for an ambush. As the buses passed, boulders and stones showered down. Every bus window was smashed. The police nevertheless re-formed and systematically drove the rioters back into the town, batonning everyone in sight, some of whom were innocent bystanders who were hounded into their homes. The 'battle' persisted from 10.30 p.m. until 3 a.m. with heavy casualties on both sides. The strike leaders claimed casualties among the police were the heavier.

The last disturbance of any significance occurred appropriately at the Ammanford No. 1 Colliery where 'blacklegs' were receiving a police escort on 7 August.

By this time events in Ammanford were attracting national interest with questions being asked in the House of Commons. Colonel Gretton (Conservative, Burton) inquired whether steps were being taken to maintain law and order. Jack Jones (Labour, Silvertown) interjected, 'Send 'em Bass's beer, that'll quieten 'em.' The Conservative Home Secretary, Joynson-Hicks, viewed the whole affair with greater concern and reported that the local police were being further augmented.

The complete breakdown of law administration and the

wholesale attack on police, colliery officials and property that occurred on 5 August must have compelled the anthracite owners to think again. Before the final agreement was reached on 22–23 August, the Combine management had already offered to reinstate Wilson if he apologised and to refer the Seniority Rule to Arbitration. These terms were rejected on 8 August by a four-to-one majority at the Anthracite District meeting. The Minority Movement throughout the coalfield began to campaign for a South Wales conference with a view to widen the industrial action. This also must have had an effect on the owners.

The agreement that facilitated the return to work on 24 August and which was recommended by the Executive Council of the SWMF included a most important concession: 'The wages and other terms and conditions prevailing at the several collieries before the stoppage [are] to continue.' The United Anthracite Company had, however, already decided not to re-open Ammanford No. 1 Colliery but undertook to make every endeavour 'to employ the workmen rendered idle … at the other collieries of the company.' The Ammanford miners were prepared to sacrifice their pit and endure short-term unemployment in order to save the Seniority Rule. In that sense, the agreement came to be seen as a momentous victory.

Retribution, however, was soon to follow. One hundred and ninety-eight miners were prosecuted and 58 of them received sentences varying from one month to eighteen months. There were wild scenes of excitement and enthusiasm throughout the trials and when prisoners were ultimately released. A shilling a week levy on all Ammanford miners allowed the payment of a minimum wage rate to all the prisoners' dependants. There were token strikes involving at least sixteen pits in the Anthracite coalfield in February 1926, as a protest against the sentences. On almost every day of the trials, busloads of miners and their families travelled to Carmarthen to cheer the prisoners, and sang hymns and the 'Red Flag' outside the courtroom, while several brass bands accompanied them. Each of the prisoners on his release was awarded a medal and a scroll by the International Class War Prisoners' Aid Society (ICWPA).

The sentences were passed in December 1925, at a time of growing national crisis inside and outside the coal industry. The Government was making detailed preparations for a General Strike. Twelve Communist leaders were imprisoned at this time and a nationwide campaign within the Labour Movement organised largely by the ICWPA coupled demands for their release with a general amnesty for the 58 miners.

The gravity of the trials and the sentences was not lost on the General Council of the Trades Union Congress which, along with the Miners' Federation of Great Britain and the Labour Party, immediately set up a fund for the dependants which, by 3 March 1926, realised over £1,000. A deputation, representing the TUC General Council, the Labour Party National Executive and the parliamentary Labour Party met the Home Secretary on 9 February 1926, to ask for clemency for the remaining prisoners. Tom Richards, general secretary of the SWMF and a member of the General Council, admitted that 'irregularities' had occurred but as the 'law had been vindicated' clemency should be considered, especially as he believed that those who were imprisoned had not been those who committed the crimes: the 'selection' process used by the police had been suspect. Similar appeals were made by Robert Smillie MP, who claimed the prisoners were not 'members of the criminal classes' but 'decent, respectable, upright and pious men'. The tenor of the appeals surprised the Home Secretary who congratulated the deputation on its 'conciliatory and very courteous' attitude. The TUC was certainly concerned about the anger in the coalfield and wished to defuse the situation. The Home Secretary, however, considered that there was something more than mere 'irregularities' at stake and after an inordinately long delay, by which time only five remained in prison, he rejected on 15 March all the requests for clemency:

> Having then, with every desire to lean on the side of mercy … I regret that I cannot see that the sentences were excessive or that in any of the cases there is ground for thinking that the verdict was mistaken and that His Majesty should for this reason be advised to remit the sentence.

The TUC was so shocked by the totality of the rejection that it pleaded with the Home Secretary not to publish the contents of the letter, obviously for fear of violence in the coalfields. The Government seemed to take one more step along a collision course that was of its own making.

Although disturbances broke out later in the inter-war period and had many of the characteristics of the anthracite struggle, none had its scale, scope and intensity.

The disturbances were undoubtedly accentuated by the ineffectiveness of the old Anthracite District of the SWMF to represent the miners of the area and to counter the strength of the new coal Combines. The strike accelerated the development of the Combine Committee whose leaders Gibbon Davies and D. B. Lewis were even appointed by the District to explain the development of the strike to the Executive Council of the SWMF. The lack of communication between the miners and their officials is clearly seen in the case of John Thomas, a miners' agent, who was apparently openly critical of the strike, and was compelled to resign. The strike revitalised the SWMF by giving momentum to the growth of a Combine Committee which was to play a leading part in the affairs of the Federation in the 1930s.

The 1925 struggle threw up its own leaders. Prominent local Communists, Ianto Evans and Arthur Thomas, as well as

Labour Party members Dai Dan Davies and Gibbon Davies set up their Combine strike committee which virtually ran the strike and inspired the disturbances. They all also played their parts in supporting the Minority Movement which was established in the area during the strike after a meeting addressed by James Griffiths and Arthur Horner.

Yet they were not a younger generation, lacking any respect for law and order. Many were older than the established District leaders and were widely respected leaders of their communities. Tom Dafen Williams, aged forty-four, was a former chairman of the Ammanford No. 2 Colliery Lodge and Dai Dan Davies was a County Alderman. Ianto Evans later became chairman of the Ammanford Rural District Council. In a testimonial sent to the Home Secretary, Elder Owen Hughes of the Cross Hands Gospel Hall, wrote of the imprisoned Edgar Lewis, with whom he was in 'close fellowship', as giving 'my heart great joy to testify to his grand moral character and Christian spirit always ready to suffer loss himself for the benefit of his follow men'.

The attack on the Seniority Rule and the coal-owners' attempt to break the strike with 'blacklegs' and police, had therefore mobilised whole anthracite communities and projected them politically leftwards. The Communist Party, in existence in Ammanford and Gwaun-Cae-Gurwen since 1920, grew in influence, membership and prestige, despite the 'warnings' of the local press, and was able to establish a branch of the Young Communist League during the strike.

The dispute, however, only intensified an already apparent socio-political development. The Great War had undoubtedly loosened the traditional deferential ties of the pit, the chapel and even the family which in the Anthracite district were perhaps not as strong as is often thought, because of the mobility of miners during the summer months. In this uncertain and receptive atmosphere, the existence of an independent working-class education in the Ammanford area contributed as something of a catalyst in preparing the miners for a major confrontation. The 'White House', set up in Ammanford by the wealthy American anarchist George Davidson, became a centre for socialist education and discussion during the war, and produced a unique group of politically conscious miners in the locality. Davidson had been influenced by Jack Griffiths (Cwmtwrch) and D. R. Owen (Garnant) who by going to the Central Labour College began a local tradition of a steady stream of anthracite miners attending the college and of establishing the Anthracite as the district with a Marxian lodge leadership of a quality that only the Rhondda could equal. Former Labour College students, particularly D. R. Owen and James Griffiths, as well as Nun Nicholas who lectured at the college for a short time, returned to take Plebs and NCLC classes and in this way politicised a hard core of miners in almost every anthracite mining village before, during and after the events of 1925.

This political trend had its repercussions on the churches and chapels. The Socialist Labour Party in Gwaun-Cae-Gurwen had in the years up to 1920 already antagonised deacons by holding their meetings on the Sabbath, while some young miners in the Garnant area attended chapel only if it was raining and then only to run a sweepstake on the first hymn. Such an anti-clerical situation became more and more pronounced during the strike. One local deacon remarked: 'There is no wonder we have our empty pews. Nothing has been said from the pulpits at Ammanford with regard to the atheism preached among the younger elements.'

More than any other disturbance in the whole inter-war period, those in the Ammanford district in 1925 saw the miners take the offensive in meeting organised police 'violence' with their own 'violence'. Colliery managers, coal-owners, newspaper reporters and police were abused and physically attacked. Even the Deputy Chief Constable of Carmarthen was beaten to within an inch of his life. One manager while on the way to his colliery was met with a typical comment: 'The only way he'll get through this picket line is on a stretcher.'

The Ammanford miners even formed a 'Defence Corps' towards the end of the strike. In this intense atmosphere of conflict and violence, the leadership of the SWMF was not exempt from using military vocabulary. S. O. Davies, who had previously worked in the Anthracite, was by 1925 the vice-president of the Federation, and in the *Sunday Worker* he called for a 'United Army'. But even more, there was scant respect for private property, a phenomenon reminiscent more of Tonypandy in 1910 than the attitudes prevailing in the inter-war period. The hundred tons of hay allegedly burnt by strikers on 5 August provided echoes of Rebecca in the county of Rebecca riots.

Yet the strikers did not rely simply on meeting violence with violence; they had their own sophisticated strategy involving espionage, sabotage, ambush, vigorous pickets and long marches. The deliberate attempts to escalate the strike immediately and so produce a short dynamic campaign was so uncharacteristic of a period that experienced protracted, unimaginative, almost predictably unsuccessful strikes. So many of the strike organisations of the time were obsessed by the necessity for a static jamboree-like atmosphere of soup kitchens and jazz bands. The strike, particularly the unique army of miners that formed a mobile picket line, scouring the Anthracite for 'blacklegs', was a refreshing interlude in the otherwise strategic desert of the 1920s. The monster picket lines, although not quite as rapid as the 1972 flying pickets, were no less effective, and remarkably afford the only practical and organisational lesson for future miners, from a period so dominated by such massive confrontations.

The sentences passed on the 58 miners outraged the sense of natural justice of the miners and their communities. At a Cross

Hands protest meeting, James Griffiths characteristically captured the feelings and social attitudes of his receptive audience:

> Let them compare young Joe Rainford getting twelve months while Hayley Morris only got three years, for ruining young working-class girls. (applause)

The miners saw it as 'naked and class justice' against their attempts to maintain their wage levels and long-established customs. The police were accused of arresting innocent bystanders, borne out by the higher number released due to lack of evidence (although the Home Office view was that this indicated the fairness of the courts). By contrast, it has been alleged that the police refused to arrest some strike leaders because they would prove to be too eloquent in court in their condemnation of the police and the owners. This argument was put forward by W. J. Davies, a young Pantyffynnon miner, who, with three others, gave themselves up at the police station after the 'Battle of Ammanford'. The police refused to arrest them. Davies claimed he 'beat up' a policeman.

Yet these miners never expected justice from a grand jury drawn from a landed proprietor class. The foreman was F. Dudley Williams-Drummond CBE, estate agent to Lord Cawdor. Also on the jury were two colonels, two majors, a captain, a knight and a parson. The severity of the sentences was considered by many miners to be an attempt to split off the militants from their communities at a time when a major conflict in the coal industry was inevitable. But the trials also saw threats to the right of free assembly. In dismissing cases against several miners for lack of evidence, the judge made an incredible statement:

> You men have had a warning. Do not congregate with others in future and be thankful for the fair way in which the prosecution has conducted your case. You may go.

The remaining disturbances from 1926 to 1936, although once again arising out of defensive actions by the miners, were on a smaller scale, were less violent, and above all, there was no kind of movement to the offensive, unlike the 1925 affair which was localised, relatively remote and totally unexpected by the authorities. The 1925 and 1926 disturbances involved miners on strike; the disturbances from 1927 to 1936 involved miners who were unemployed, an important and fundamental difference. Yet there was one common denominator to all the disturbances: the age structure of the rioters. The average age of the Ammanford rioters was over thirty-one and is approximately the same for all the other disturbances, which discounts any question of mere youthful exuberance. At the Pantyffynnon Colliery disturbance, the average age of the arrested rioters was 39.4 years.

The anthracite strike and riots were part of a unique thread running through the trade union activities of the South Wales miners in the 1920s and 1930s. It was part syndicalist and part a belief in the righteousness and effectiveness of direct action. The riots, disturbances, strikes, street demonstrations, hunger marches, social ostracism of 'scabs', stay-down strikes, along with the willingness to suffer prison sentences as well as the volunteering to fight Fascism in Spain, were all part of this tradition.

Turmoil and trouble apart, the steadfastness of the mass of the anthracite miners secured the Seniority Rule. This achievement alone was sufficient to insulate the whole of the Anthracite District against the whittling away of the Miners' Federation which occurred so dramatically elsewhere in the South Wales coalfield and in all the other British coalfields. Victimisation of militants by the coal-owners with the return to work at the end of 1926 was made virtually impossible in the Anthracite, which became the haven for a few victimised Rhondda miners, notably Arthur Horner and Jack Jones. Several of the leading Anthracite propagandists, many of whom had won their spurs in the battles of 1925, were also recruited into the eastern part of the South Wales coalfield in the mid-1930s to crush the 'scab' union at Taff Merthyr and Bedwas.

The anthracite miners undoubtedly became the backbone of the SWMF and this was very much to do with the securing of the Seniority Rule in 1925.

3

The Secret World of the South Wales Miner: The Relevance of Oral History*

Before 1640, the traditions I have been describing (Lollardy, Anabaptism, etc.) circulated verbally. Historians, themselves the products of a literary culture, relying so much on written or printed evidence, are always in danger of underestimating verbal transmission of ideas.

– Christopher Hill (1978)

Oh we ran [pit papers in Aberdare in the 1920s] for about a year or more. And I don't know where they went to – you never kept them you see. In the Movement I never kept anything you see. We worked from day to day … We never thought of keeping a diary or mind if I had kept a diary it would have been very good now … And, of course, my political understanding was not high at the time really. You built up over a period and there's much implication of things I didn't fully understand, I understood them a little perhaps.

– Max Goldberg (6 September 1972 interview, South Wales Miners' Library)

---

* First published in David Smith (ed.), *A People and a Proletariat: Essays in the History of Wales 1780–1980* (Pluto Press, 1980).

THE IMPORTANCE OF ORAL testimony to the contemporary social historian is now undisputed. The use that is made of it, however, can be highly controversial: in the absence of traditional manuscript material, it can simply be a substitute and often an invaluable one. More often it supplements other sources wherever they are inadequate. The aim of this essay is to suggest that there is a qualitative difference in oral evidence as a source and that material already available on the South Wales coalfield amply indicates this. Furthermore, the methodology adopted to collect such material and its analysis afford some important clues in the tracing of an evolving class – if not proletarian – consciousness among the working people of the South Wales mining valleys. It is this last question which provides the core of my enquiry: what kind of understanding do we have of the creation of what can be described as a unique proletarian coalfield society in the twentieth century and how was this particular collectivist consciousness forged?

For the historian of the twentieth century to ignore oral evidence is tantamount to taking a decision to write off whole areas of human experience. Indeed, there are human activities which can only satisfactorily be uncovered by collecting oral testimony. Most societies have their secret worlds whether out of necessity because of their clandestine, semi-legal or illegal qualities or because there is no written tradition as Jan Vansina has shown is the case amongst African tribes. (Secret in the sense that Western observers are orientated away from the importance of collective, received memory.) But even in such an advanced, reasonably literate, industrial society as the mining valleys of South Wales between the wars, with its range of social and political institutions each spawning a multiplicity of primary and secondary historical sources, there is a world beyond this which is not, and cannot be, analysed or even chronicled without the intervention of oral testimony. It is only concealed because the historian may choose to ignore the value of human memory.

Where do we, for example, find evidence of child labour in the South Wales coalfield in the early part of the twentieth century? What kind of perceptive insight do we get of Aberdare in the 1900s from Max Goldberg?

> I had to work from when I was eight years of age. I worked in a barber's shop every night except a Tuesday night, and from eight o'clock Saturday morning until twelve o'clock Saturday night. I was so small I used to stand on the box to lather the men's faces you know, and I used to get one and six a week for that and the man I worked for, he was so bad he used to make me, you know when I went in to have my tea, I had to have it standing up … I used to go up to the toilet to have a little rest you know and I used to cry you know. I remember crying, I would be tired out you know. So I left there, and then I worked in a grocer's and I had to work the same every evening and then Saturday all day and I got half a crown a week then. So it was a big help in the house you see.

How many historians would consider the last sentence to be the most important of the testimony? Does the detail of exploitation transcend the final judgement of the narrator? Similarly, Jim Evans' boyhood experience in the Rhymney Valley during the First World War is again something of a revelation and gives an added dimension to war-time food shortages:

> [I] started work in the Post Office as a telegram boy. I had been working for three years prior to that carrying out for the grocer: went down in the morning before school, sweeping out the shop, putting the sawdust down, delivering little orders on the way to school. Go down in the lunch hour again to see if there were any orders, then after going home, having tea and go to the grocer's and work until eight o'clock, nine o'clock in the night … Half a crown and an egg was my weekly wage but they were very, very

meticulous about the egg. They used to shake it and make sure it was a good one because I was a good errand boy.

Such an accumulation of evidence gives a better understanding not only of social conditions but of the history of the class itself. The extent to which this very early work experience contributed to a personal appreciation of exploitation as a class phenomenon is much more of a central question than whether the working class in general was ever psychologically conditioned by 'go, and do thou likewise'.

The discovery of such unchronicled experiences applies even more forcibly, and in a universal sense, to women. Where, other than through oral testimony, can the historian trace the industrial and domestic work experience of women in this century in the mining valleys of South Wales? A remarkable diversity, progressing from a variety of mining jobs (surface and underground) to employment in tinworks, brickworks, ammunition and clock factories, were all encompassed in the first five decades of this century in but one mining locality – Ystradgynlais. This was apart from working on farms, in local shops, pubs, hotels and 'gwasanaethu' (domestic service) outside their own homes, in the immediate area and beyond.

The whole distorted experience of South Wales in the inter-war period is one which can easily be misinterpreted by the social historian. Oral testimony can very often be the only corrective.

The demise of young women, trapped in a male-oriented, economically depressed society, evades the grasp of the historian, usually because there are no obvious sources. How, for example, do we adequately trace that seemingly subterranean network which tapped the limitless cheap female labour market within the coalfield and resulted in that army of Welsh domestic servants in the Home Counties? It is only by talking to such people that we begin to put flesh on the statistical bones which indicate the mammoth population changes between 1871 and 1951, particularly in the Rhondda. To understand coalfield society we must not only scrutinise Hunger Marching Tonypandy miners but also Mardy girls in service in Croydon in the 1920s:

> And they just received me from this girl and in I went; I felt awfully nervous and then she took me to my bedroom which was right up in the attic and told me to change into my afternoon uniform and to come down to make tea. Well if I hadn't been to this training centre; I wouldn't know the difference between afternoon tea and high tea, because we didn't have that kind of thing at home … They were both widows, the daughter had two sons, the older son which I called Mr Eric and the younger was Master Kenneth. They were supposed to be very religious people and I suppose they were. Anyway evening times we used to have a cooked meal and I would take my plate and have whatever was going. I never really had enough you know but I would never ask for more. I was too frightened to ask for more … I didn't feel I was part of the family at all. I felt I was the servant then you know and I was there to do my work and that was that … they didn't converse much with me at all, and when they did it was just to run the Welsh down … You wouldn't say that they were gentry because I met gentry after that and I found that they were far better; nicer people than they were.

But what of the complexities of class and nationality in faraway London society as seen through the eyes of the same Rhondda girl in service in a Clapham Common Welsh dairy?

> We used to go quite a lot on a Sunday evening after Chapel up to Hyde Park to the Welsh Corner there and we used to meet people from home and we used to have a wonderful time chatting and having news from home … There was a London Welsh Society because my master and mistress belonged to it, because they used

to have luncheons and things, periodically you know, and they used to dress up. And I used to love to watch them dressing and I used to help the daughter, and I never went to anything like this. Mind you, they were very kind if there was any dramas or anything … I used to go with them by car.

Indeed, central to an understanding of this hidden world is the question of class (a theme which appears in all the above testimonies). The emergence of a proletariat should not be measured only (if at all) by the collation of statistical evidence on parliamentary elections. Even within a seemingly homogeneous workforce moulded by a fairly straightforward economy there are complexities of race, language, religion, urbanisation, parochial loyalties, internal and external labour mobility, population movements and depths of class hostility in which oral testimony is either the only historical source or is the major indicator. (This is to say nothing of the effect upon valleys and communities of uneven economic development, private ownership patterns and differences in the quality of coal.) Furthermore, oral evidence very often gives a completely different insight into defining a working class. The quality of its consciousness is the interaction of so many variable strands: loyalty to such organisations as the Labour Party, the South Wales Miners' Federation or the Communist Party can often only be expressions of finely developed class instincts which manifest themselves in many other ways and whose roots are not always simple.

The semi-rural anthracite mining village of Abercraf in the Upper Swansea Valley is a classic example. It was one of the last pit villages in which the owners were not one or other of the massive coal Combines, but families who lived locally. Their social and economic control was diffused and apparently all-embracing. The class tensions and relationships were liable, consequently, to be intense and perverse. One miner recalled:

The Morgans' and the Davies' … they were coal-owners and they had such big families, big followings you know. And I mean; you couldn't open your mouth in that colliery without it was carried back you know … If they [the union] had a meeting, they [the owners] had their cronies coming to the meeting, and you'd know it would be out straight and back to the colliery owner … Now those [miners] as a family … and good workmen all of them … exceptionally good men with an 'atchet … [one of the brothers] could kill a pig … He'd learnt that amount of trade although he was a miner trained … and, of course, he had these tools of a butcher, sharp knives, saw. And this under-manager … was playing around with other women you see, and this [miner] was living next door to one woman that he was carrying on with. And he made a statement to that effect. And now this under-manager was coming down this road, and he pulled him up and he said 'Listen now, you keep your mouth shut about me' … And one thing went from another, he waves his stick and he was going to hit [the miner] see. [The miner] stuck him with a knife … They took the case to the Assizes … and [he] was let off pretty lenient … But the renegades in Waunclawdd [Colliery] when he was jailed for six months, these men … said 'Listen, we've got a butty now in jail and he done the right thing, a thing that a good many of us would have done … What about his wife and kiddies?' So we rose a levy in the lodge, as long as [he] was in jail … we decided to pay [his wife] the minimum wage. He came out and he thanked us … well they're both dead now . . . and then when his [the under-manager's] retirement came, he was ignored by the people in the village, and he felt it. He was a sorry sight, he was a capable man … he was a well-spoken man, but he loaned himself to them, he was there only to make profits for the company.

Received oral tradition in the late 1970s relates that the same under-manager would insist that his chapel's programme for the annual *cymanfa ganu* (religious singing festival) would have a hymn which included the following verse:

Er imi dwyllo'r byd
A llwyddo i guddio mai
Rwy'n chwerw 'mron; er hyn i gyd
Nid yw'm heuogrwydd lai.

[Although I have deceived the world
And succeeded in covering my faults
I have a bitter breast; despite all this
My guilt is none the less.]

It is significant in itself that the memory of this small episode should have survived for over half a century. In such a relatively self-contained community, whose class structure was fairly simple, two important and inter-related phenomena had a profound effect on a sharpening class, trade-union and political consciousness amongst the workforce between the wars. Without the use of oral testimony, the full extent of these influences would be difficult to assess.

Firstly, the teaching of Marxism under the banner of the National Council of Labour Colleges (NCLC), as elsewhere, undoubtedly helped to challenge the consensus, 'community', notions perpetrated by village elders, whether they be coal-owners, their officials, chapel deacons or ageing lodge officers. The classes, conducted particularly by such an irreverent tutor as Nun Nicholas, bred a new generation of miners' leaders in the locality which partly resulted in members of the village playing a disproportionately large role in the wider affairs of the South Wales Miners' Federation (SWMF) and later the South Wales area of the National Union of Mineworkers (NUM). That one of the lodges in the village was expelled from the SWMF for a period during the Second World War in no way diminishes this long-term contribution, although the enduring bitterness caused by the expulsion is measurable in a negative sense by the lack of oral evidence. Like family skeletons, past union disgrace can be erased from the collective memory.

Secondly, the small Spanish community which arrived, via Dowlais in 1911, had a leavening effect on industrial militancy in the area and particularly within the two local lodges of Abercraf and International. Oral tradition has it that they were the best trade unionists. One lodge secretary, who along with most of his generation in the village was considerably influenced by the uncomplicated philosophy of the hard-working Spaniards, was Dai Dan Evans:

> I've never found any Spaniard in arrears with his union contribution … A shilling a fortnight, you could bank upon the Spaniards coming there to pay their contributions. And whenever there was a ballot held, they used to go on to the secretary and ask him – 'Which of these is the Communist?' 'Comunista', they said. Their vote was invariably to the Communist candidate.

Other dimensions of this unequivocal philosophy constantly burst through in this small ethnic community which took such great pride in its received historical tradition. A second generation Abercraf Spaniard recalled his father's outlook:

> 'The Sermon on the Mount, can you beat it?' he used to tell me … it was pure socialism. But organised religion was quite a different thing altogether. So what he said was this, 'If you don't learn anything bad by going to Sunday school or going to a church, or to a chapel, all right, fair enough, you can go.' And the priests used to come round and try to get us to go to the Catholic church which was then down in Pontardawe. And he used to say … 'No, why should my children go all the way down to Pontardawe, when there's a church round the corner … if God is in your church, surely he must be in this church as well.' And for people who were being brought up, steeped in Catholicism, I think this was a very progressive way of thinking. And this was the philosophy we had at home. It was a philosophy of what I considered to be true socialism … It was practised in the house you lived in. And, of course, in those days … you sat round the

fire at night and you had your old story telling. My grandfather, my grandmother, my father and my mother, they used to tell us stories they had learned as children themselves round their fires in Spain as little children. So we learned through these stories, we learned the history of Spain, we learned about all the folk-lore of the parts of the country they lived in.

They took such philosophical values into the colliery. On seeing the under-manager spit in the face of a submissive collier one Spaniard was heard to say, 'If he did that in Spain, cemetery for him.' Their attitude towards the colliery owners was nothing short of contemptuous and must have eroded the lingering effects of paternalism in the village: that their utterances are recalled over sixty years later is surely evidence of that. One group of young Spanish miners, on being criticised by the manager for not working regularly, are said to have replied: 'We've earned enough for our week's keep: food, for our lodge, and for our beer – they're not exploiting us any more.'

The complexity of working-class politicisation and its relationship with particular immigrant groups is a question of crucial importance to an understanding of the dynamics of South Wales society in the early part of the twentieth century. What qualitative change occurred with the influx of Caernarvonshire quarrymen, Cardiganshire and Somerset farm-hands into the coalfield? What were the manifold inter-relationships between the groups and between them and the receiving community? Did they merge immediately or did they try to emulate the success of Irish Catholics (as in Maesteg, Merthyr and Mountain Ash) and the Spaniards of Abercraf and Dowlais, by creating something of a community within a community?

Ben 'Sunshine' Davies recalls the impact of Rhondda life upon him in 1919. It was as if he was moving from one timescale to another: leaping out of a remote, closed, almost feudal rural society, still dominated by the religiosity of a Nonconformist chapel which shut the only village pub soon after the Revival, into a twentieth-century world:

> Well I think it was around the end of August or September we decided to leave Cardigan for Ferndale. I was at present serving on a farm on the cliffs of New Quay, a farm called Penbryn farm. I can well recall it was the beginning of the corn harvest and I had difficulty in extracting myself from my service with the farm but by a lot of arguments I did manage to get myself free to travel with my mother and my brothers to Ferndale with a view of starting underground as there was a demand for miners immediately after the war … I started … at the age of sixteen … I went as a butty to a Bristol chap by the name of George Cheetham, and he was very, very deep Bristol brogue with him and I was very Welshy, didn't speak much English in Cardigan although I could understand, but to express myself after was a bit difficult and especially with this person from Bristol. But as time wore on we became more acquainted with our discourse and we were able to communicate very well … My mother found that I was a bit homesick … I was given a holiday back to the country, Whitsun the following year. And after that visit back home I had a week's holiday and then the longing seemed to wear off because there was a lot of attraction in Ferndale … There was picture houses, then there was plenty of dramas and theatres again in the Workmen's Hall … and a nice billiard place there, bars to go into, a nice reading room … I found it very strange the first day that I went down [underground]. After reaching the pit bottom we walked down into the darkness with a little oil lamp and we were all having a 'spell' … And there they were chatting and explaining their differences and touching on different topics, some economics, others politics, others about their domestic troubles … I was astonished to hear such a lot of mixed arguments and people trying to explain things – some in Welsh, others in English, and we were boys then sitting altogether and listening attentively.

It was the same kind of tempestuous environment which

Maximilian Stanislav Goldberg saw in Aberdare during the Great War. Undoubtedly, the receiving community shaped his rebellious outlook but it was his Irish Catholic roots which sparked his interest in revolutionary politics:

> Well I was for Ireland. My mother was Irish and in the Church. I got linked up with Irish chaps so I thought Irish. I didn't have any real political understanding but I thought Ireland was being badly done by and therefore I lent my support to this. I joined the Irish Self-Determination League. It was the sort of counterpart to the Movement that was very active in Ireland … Well we held meetings and discussions and there used to be, if we could get any gunpowder or stuff like that we used to get it if we could, to send across … Yes, this was the beginning.

Out of Aberdare and Merthyr came the largest groups of Welsh volunteers for the International Brigades: arguably the highest form of proletarian consciousness. Within these groups, perhaps surprisingly, were many lapsed Catholics of Irish origin. Certainly when the historian also examines the major Irish contribution to the development of working-class organisations in many urban centres in South Wales, the roots of the Labour Movement are by no means only Radical Nonconformity (if at all).

In stark contrast to the dynamic cosmopolitan qualities of the central and eastern Valleys, the rural anthracite coalfield to the west experienced a much slower rate of proletarianisation, largely reflecting the leisurely pace of economic development. The divide within the coalfield is highlighted by the perceptive observation of an anthracite miner:

> [Caerlan] was a small community of about twenty-eight houses including a farmhouse, a grocer, a barber's shop and a public house. It was at the top end of the Swansea Valley and … its ideas were polarised between two institutions, the chapel and the public

house. It was on the periphery of the coalfield … and that made it a very unique place so far as a large number of men who were working in the pits had their roots in the agricultural areas and therefore had not been proletarianised in the same way as the heart of the South Wales coalfield … You had some men with dual loyalties, loyalties to their old ideas … as farmers … Life to us in the Rhondda was exceedingly artificial … There was no trees on the mountains; all the animals that you had were domestic animals … There is not a farm to be seen anywhere … The tink of the damn pit, the tink of the tramcars on the road, that's all you would hear. Rhondda people are acclimatised to what I would say now is a very uncouth proletarian life … in the sense that there is nothing natural about it … people were clustered one on top of the other, you see, one road, the road and the river took the whole of the bottom of the valley.

At the very time Max Goldberg and Ben 'Sunshine' were entering the Aberdare and Rhondda valleys, the tightly-knit anthracite villages gave a different meaning to the 'all-Welsh rule', the closed-shop and to 'community politics':

Cymraeg oedd pawb yn siarad yn y pentre, oedd dim Saeson wedi dod. Os fydde Sais yn dod 'ma, fydde chi'n gofyn i ambell i hen ddyn, 'Pwy yw'r dyn na, chi'n nabod e?' 'O nagw i, man from off somewhere.' Dyn diarth. A cofiwch oedd gofyn bod e'n cered yn weddol o gwmws, 'se dynon diarth yr amser hynny, a gwŷr Cwmtwrch a gwŷr Cwmllynfell, oe'n nhw'n parochial iawn, oedd dim lot o groeso i ddyn diarth … Gwedwch, hyd yn oed rhywun, na nhad i chi. Dod o Gwm Nedd, i Gwmtwrch. Dyn dwad oedd e chi'n gweld, oedd e'm yn native, oedd e ddim wedi ei eni a'i fagu yng Nghwmtwrch. Oedd gofyn bod chi wedi cael eich geni a'ch magu yma cyn bod chi'n un o wŷr Cwmtwrch neu Cwmllynfell. Os fydde chi'n dod o Gwynfe, neu fel oe'n i'n gweud wrthoch chi, Aberdâr neu rywle, oedd un dyn yn gweud wrth nhad, 'Cadw lygad ar hwnna, dim lot o olwg ar hwnna.' A'n enwedig os oedd e'n siarad Saesneg. Oedd e fod i chael hi, fights mawr yn

Cwmtwrch yn amser 'ny chi'n gweld, oedd hi'n amser garw iawn yn Cwmtwrch. O, a cicio, oe'n nhw'n leicio cicio, fel ma nhw yn Yorkshire a Lancashire, os nag oe nhw'n gallu wado nhw ar eu dwylo, cwpwl o bunts oe nhw'n gael chi'n gweld, bechgyn diarth. Wedyn oedd gofyn bod nhw'n iwso'u pennau neu oe nhw ddim yn para'n hir 'ma.

[Welsh was spoken by everybody in the village, there were no Englishmen. If an Englishman came here, you'd ask an old man, 'Who is that man, do you know him?' 'Oh no I don't, man from off somewhere.' A stranger. And remember it was necessary that he toed the line fairly well, if they were strangers, in those days, men from Cwmtwrch and men from Cwmllynfell, they were very parochial. There wasn't very much welcome for a stranger; say even someone, there's my father for you. Came from the Neath Valley to Cwmtwrch. [About fifteen miles.] He was a man who came in you see, he wasn't a native, he wasn't born and bred in Cwmtwrch. You had to be born and bred here before you were one of the people of Cwmtwrch or Cwmllynfell. If you came from Gwynfe, or as I was saying to you, Aberdare or somewhere, one man would say to my father, 'Keep an eye on him, I don't think much of him.' And especially if he spoke English. He was in for it, big fights in Cwmtwrch in those days you see. It was a very rough time in Cwmtwrch. Oh, and kicking, they liked to kick, as they do in Yorkshire and Lancashire, if they couldn't beat them with their hands, they'd have a couple of kicks you see, the strangers. Then it was important that they used their heads or they didn't last long here.]

Even into the 1930s non-Welsh-speaking Welshmen from Abergavenny or Merthyr were considered English, and would have great difficulty in obtaining work in Cwmtwrch or Cwmllynfell collieries. Such apparent insularity (or was it working-class self-defence?) survived down to the late 1950s:

But when the pit actually closed [in 1959] we had an Englishman on the Committee, and then we'd revert to English. But when the colliery was at its best they were even conducting the Annual

Meeting and General Meetings in Cwmtwrch and Cwmllynfell Hall, every other in turns, and they would conduct all their affairs in Welsh even if the English were there.

The complexity of getting a 'start' at such collieries seemed to have the parochial support of owners and men:

When there was a shortage of labour in Cwmllynfell Colliery, they employed a few extra from Cwmtwrch, not enough men say in Cwmllynfell village to man the pit, so they were having extra labour from Cwmtwrch. When there was more shortage after that, they were having men from Ystalyfera providing they could play in the Cwmllynfell band. And the Cwmtwrch people were having jobs in Brynhenllys and Cwmtwrch at one time providing they were prepared to pay Dr Owen [the Cwmtwrch doctor who had shareholdings at a local colliery].

The extent to which such local customs and agreements were significant in holding back a more worldly perspective is difficult to assess. But in examining the industrial relations of the anthracite coalfield in the first decade of nationalisation, they cannot be ignored. Hidden, unwritten agreements between managers and men to deceive the coal-owner had to come out now that the National Coal Board had come into being. One manager recalled such attitudes as:

'Well I'm looking after my men, I'll treat them in the way I want to treat them, not what the coal-owners … want to do, see … ' And that is the difficulty we found in the Anthracite after nationalisation was to sort things out.

But even such apparently enduring localised attitudes had been eroded by internal mobility between the anthracite and the steam coalfields. The extent of 'tramping', and its contribution to the breakdown of anthracite isolation is difficult to measure. But as with George Ewart Evans' discovery of those farm labourers who followed their barley to Burton-on-Trent, it needs an oral historian to ask the first questions and often to get the first answers.

'There are no Christians in Banwen' was an utterance, redolent with local nuance, used by a pit manager to describe a workforce which aspired to shake off its deference to its 'betters'.

Nothing could have been more appropriate. It is a statement which begs particular questions about the nature of all those communities across the coalfield in which the working class was now emerging in the early part of the twentieth century. To deny its different rates of retardation and development, its ethnic, regional and local roots is to deny it has a history at all.

Bibliographical note

All the interviews quoted in this essay are transcribed tape recordings deposited at the South Wales Miners' Library in Swansea University. They were collected (with one exception) by the Social Science Research Council financed South Wales Coalfield History Project during the period 1972–74. Leandro Macho's testimony was a recorded lecture at the Library entitled 'Growing up in Spanish Abercraf in the 1930s'. The interviews were of Ben 'Sunshine' Davies (Banwen), Dai Dan Evans (Cae'r-Lan, Abercraf), Jim Evans (Abercraf), David Francis (Onllwyn), Max Goldberg (Aberdare), Josiah Jones [Joe 'Brickman'] (Cwmllynfell), Will 'Post' Rees (Cwmtwrch), Jim Vale (Abercraf), John Williams (Banwen) and Maria Williams (Mardy). The collection is almost entirely transcribed and indexed and has a very wide range of recollections on the South Wales coalfield in the twentieth century with special emphasis on male and female work experience, trade-union, political and workers' educational activities, anti-fascism, the Spanish Civil War, the 1926 lockout and migration into the Valleys at the turn of this century. The project's final report (1974) gives a full account of its oral history programme. A further project, also financed by the SSRC, began in 1979 with the aim of collecting sound and video tapes on the period since 1945 within the coalfield.

Apart from historians of the late nineteenth and twentieth centuries, Christopher Hill is one of the very few who has given any attention to the significance of received oral tradition. His essay 'From Lollards to Levellers' in Maurice Cornforth (ed.), *Rebels and their Causes: Essays in Honour of A. L. Morton* (1978) has important insights.

The pioneer in the field of British oral history is George Ewart Evans, some of whose work on the South Wales miners is published in *From Mouths of Men* (1976). The first concerted exercise in the collecting of oral evidence in Wales was made by the Welsh Folk Museum under the guidance of Vincent Phillips. Although it has concentrated on folklore, rural society and the Welsh language, it has accumulated some important material on coal mining. In particular, Lynn Davies' pamphlet *Aspects of Mining Folklore in Wales* (reprinted from *Folk Life* 9) and his *Geirfa Glöwr* (1976) – the Miner's Vocabulary – are both valuable studies.

The most prominent British academic in the field in this early period of oral history was Dr Paul Thompson of the University of Essex, whose *The Voice of the Past: Oral History* (1978) is a comprehensive survey of oral history work throughout the world. It is also the best account of the importance of oral testimony to the social historian. He has a much simpler explanation of methodology than the nonetheless erudite *Oral Tradition* (1965) by Jan Vansina which focuses more exclusively on African tribal societies. Dr Thompson was also the editor of *Oral History*, the journal of the British Oral History Society which continues to publish articles, conference reports and work in progress.

Amongst the most productive British groups have been the

Centerprise Publishing Project which has concentrated on the community history of the East End.

During the period I was researching this essay a considerable amount of oral evidence was used in the social and labour history of the South Wales coalfield some of which was published in *Llafur,* the journal of the Society for the Study of Welsh Labour History. Two theses which relied heavily on such testimony were Kim Howells', *A View from Tradition, Experience and Nationalisation in the South Wales Coalfield 1937–1957* (University of Warwick, 1979) and my own, *The South Wales Miners and the Spanish Civil War: A Study in Internationalism* (University of Wales, 1977). *The Fed: A History of the South Wales Miners in the Twentieth Century* (1980) by David Smith and myself also makes considerable use of miners' recollections.

American coalfield historians have long used oral testimony including *Patch/Work Voices: The Culture and Lore of a Mining People* (1977) by Dennis F. Brestensky, Evelyn A. Hovanec and Albert N. Skomra, all of the Fayette campus of Pennsylvania State University. Video and sound recording has also figured prominently in the work of the Highlander Research and Educational Center (Tennessee) which has links with the South Wales Miners' Library. The Center published Matt Witt's *In Our Blood* (1979) which is an account of four American coalmining families who are the sons and daughters of European immigrants, of black field hands from the South, and Navajo Indians.

4

Mining the
Popular Front*

THE BRITISH MINERS' STRIKE of 1984–85 has raised some fundamental questions concerning the nature of industrial and political alliances. In particular, the Welsh experience may offer some useful lessons beyond the NUM and beyond the strike. The South Wales coalfield, with over 20,000 miners, has remained solid in support of the NUM's fight for jobs, pits and communities: after ten months barely 1 per cent had broken the strike and in the fourteen central valleys only fourteen people had returned to work by mid-January. By contrast, however, support in the small North Wales coalfield (only two pits and less than 2,000 men) was always patchy and virtually collapsed overnight in November.

The emergence in Wales of a broad democratic alliance of possibly a new kind – an anti-Thatcher alliance – is not the reason for this resistance. But an examination of its origins and development will perhaps begin to explain the intensity of the phenomenon. The Wales Congress in Support of Mining Communities grew out of a linked realisation that in order to feed miners' families more efficiently and in order to explain the case for coal more effectively, greater unity was needed. But what

---

* First published in *Marxism Today*, February 1985.

was also important was that it was a *political* realisation, born out of necessity within the miners' struggle, and arrived at virtually simultaneously by several political, trade union, cultural and other organisations.

When the Wales Congress in Support of Mining Communities was launched in Cardiff's City Hall on 21 October to consolidate and broaden support for the NUM's strike throughout Wales, its proceedings were dramatically interrupted by sixty London local government workers marching in with a banner proclaiming 'Brent Nalgo supports the Dulais Valley'.

The following week a large contingent of gays and lesbians were in the Dulais Valley as guests of miners' families because of their outstanding fundraising for the miners' cause. A short time later food arrived in West Wales from the Greenham Common women who had earlier in the strike been entertained by a South Wales striking miners' choir.

Even earlier in the year the sedate calm of respectable Wales, absorbing its annual dose of culture at the National Eisteddfod, was broken by public meetings on the Eisteddfod field in support of the miners. Farmers, church leaders, teachers, public employees, Welsh language activists, historians, poets, folksingers, communists, members of the Labour Party and Plaid Cymru, ministers of religion, the women's movement and the peace movement all made common cause in support of Welsh mining communities.

Out of this remarkable and new unity on the Eisteddfod field and a myriad of other new alliances elsewhere, grew the Wales Congress. Such seemingly unlikely and unexpected alliances could never have been expected by Nicholas Ridley MP when he drew up his secret anti-union and anti-strike plans in 1978, which anticipated major industrial strikes but did not foresee broad popular support for such struggles.

What is the political significance of these new alliances forged during the miners' strike across and beyond the British coalfields and does the Wales Congress, in particular, represent a 'new politics'? Or will it all fade away with the end of this 'exceptional' industrial struggle?

Throughout the late summer of 1984 the NUM leadership was understandably preparing to maximise its support at the TUC and Labour Party conferences in the autumn.

But the real business of struggle and survival was going on elsewhere. For one reason or another, and now with the benefit of hindsight, we can truthfully say that Eric Hammond of the EEPTU was right: the trade union movement, with the glorious exception of the railway workers, has not delivered the goods when and where it matters. This is not to say that there have not been magnificent collections and tremendous public demonstrations. But Christmas parties and food parcels alone, important as they are, do not win public support, let alone achieve power cuts.

Alliances

Old-fashioned trade union solidarity has, at best, been reduced to 75 turkeys from Llanwern steelworkers. At its worst, it's the army of well-paid faceless scab lorry drivers trundling daily along the M4 to supply foreign coke to the Llanwern 'brothers' who supplied the turkeys. That is the reality of an industrial battle which relies essentially on what amounts to no more than a 'syndicalist' strategy of industrial confrontation and regular sectional calls for a general strike and mass picketing to resolve the situation. Fortunately, the miners' strike in every coalfield has been far more than that – it had to be because of the inadequacy of the Triple Alliance and the ineffectiveness of the TUC in enforcing Congress decisions.

Nevertheless there is no doubt that the miners' struggle has often been conducted as if we were living in those far-off days of industrial militancy in the early 1970s – successful mass and flying pickets, workers' occupations and unemployment at less than a million. It was the era of unity of transport workers and miners on picket lines which gave birth to the Wales TUC.

One other factor is forgotten about that period. Even though the two strikes of 1972 and 1974 were of relatively short duration, the victories were not achieved by industrial action and industrial solidarity alone. Despite power cuts, the miners won broad public support which ultimately led to the fall of the Heath Government.

There was broad support even if it did not develop into tangible broad alliances. Since then the trade union movement has been debilitated by mass unemployment, impotent TUC leadership, the Thatcherite ideological offensive and successive state assaults, from Grunwick through to the NGA, on its very existence.

Until the present miners' strike, the movement had been in retreat for years. In the summer of 1980, in the wake of the first Thatcherite onslaught on the steelworkers, the industrial correspondent of *The Times* wrote that we were about to witness the most severe testing of the 'shock-troops of the labour movement' – the South Wales miners. Some observers had already written them off. Others predicted their skirmishes in defence of jobs and communities in 1981 and 1983. But what no one could have anticipated was the intensity and ferocity of the state onslaught on the British miners in 1984 and the manner in which they successfully withstood it.

That survival, that resistance, is encapsulated in the words of an old Cynon Valley miner: 'After the experience of the last ten months, the miners and their communities have learnt how to survive together – they shouldn't ever have to fear the prospect of unemployment again.'

Even more perceptive and revealing was the simple ceremony in Italy during the strike when women activists from Coelbren and Hirwaun were made honorary members of the Italian resistance. In a period when the NUM is being attacked by every arm of the state, it is not an exaggeration to say that the union is about to be driven underground. The freezing of South Wales miners' funds through sequestration in August was part of this process. The subsequent survival of the union in South Wales inevitably begs certain questions.

A resistance movement

In the Welsh context, the nearest historical comparison we can make with the events of 1984–5 within communities and valleys is the broad unity and resistance during the miners' lockout of 1926 and in the mid-1930s on the questions of struggle over mass unemployment, scab unionism and aid for Republican Spain. At that time, class and community converged, significantly enough at a time of trade union weakness. *Mining* communities were becoming or had become *unemployed* communities and their struggles even embraced chapels and shopkeepers. Such struggles were essentially extra-parliamentary in character and involved the mobilisation of whole communities.

But that socio-political unity was transient and despite the courage of exceptional Labour leaders like Aneurin Bevan the broad-based unity around the South Wales Council of Action of 1935–6 was broken by the anti-communism of right-wing trade union and Labour leaders who saw Labourism as the rightful monolith in the Valleys. Historical links there are. The strong sense of solidarity and the organic relationship between union, community and pit is still so intense that it cannot be dismissed simply as blind loyalty to be 'lauded by future trade union historians' as South Wales area director Philip Weekes remarked when the anticipated return to work in South Wales again failed to materialise in the New Year.

However, it would be much more fruitful for our purposes

to examine our immediate past in order to understand the developments which led up to the Wales Congress. There is no doubt that in many respects the Wales Congress might be seen as only a *formalisation* of what also exists to an extent in all the other striking British coalfields, the most significant feature of which is the creation (as in 1926 but much more successfully now – partly because there are fewer miners) of an alternative welfare system. Put more sharply it is a *resistance* movement. The way striking mining communities have responded to the threat to their very existence has been the most remarkable feature of the strike. This socio-political development is undoubtedly part of the same phenomenon that resists rate-capping in local government; that opposes the abolition of the GLC and other metropolitan bodies; the mobilising of the unemployed around the People's March for Jobs; and the mass peace campaigns against Cruise and Trident. In that sense they are all extra-parliamentary struggles which place greater emphasis than hitherto on educating and mobilising communities and organisations in broad alliances.

In a Welsh context, it is part of the same process that saw in the early 1980s the women's anti-nuclear march from Cardiff to Greenham Common; the Welsh Language Society campaigning against unemployment because without work, the Welsh language will die; Valley parents involving themselves in direct action to oppose cuts in school bus services (including the setting up of an alternative school); and Valley communities uniting with NUPE members to oppose hospital closures.

The common threads in all these struggles were the tactic of non-violent civil disobedience; the mobilising of people beyond the traditional parameters of the labour movement; and most important of all, the mobilising of whole communities in their own defence.

Unifying the threads

What the MacGregor NCB closures announcement in March 1984 did was to accelerate these trends and ultimately force their convergence. To say that the 'women against pit closures' movement suddenly transformed women's attitudes is to misunderstand the processes which had already been operating in mining communities. The Greenham Common protest was started by working-class women in the Rhondda. Very many of the women active in the 1984–85 struggle were already prominently involved in politics and the peace movement at a local level.

Furthermore, the Welsh Language Society had already made the link with workers in struggle well before the miners' strike. People and organisations were therefore already making connections: they were already identifying allies and enemies.

What the miners' strike in all the coalfields did was to begin to bring such developments together, involving now not just single communities or groups of activities but whole regions and tens of thousands of people. It is also something beyond that. This new kind of alternative welfare system has created in many places a very resilient and tough resistance movement.

Everyone should now acknowledge that the network of women and mixed support groups has given rise to an alternative, community-based system of food, clothing, financial *and* morale distribution which has sustained about half a million people for nearly a year. The social and political skills of organisation and communication are akin to the experiences of people during a social revolution. Women, men and indeed children have learnt more about the strengths and weaknesses of the state apparatus, more about the problems of building working-class solidarity and, above all, more about their own individual and collective human potential than at any time in their lives. The new links within and between coalfields, with non-mining areas in

Britain and indeed internationally are all pregnant with political possibilities.

What emerges is a network of unexpected alliances which go far beyond the traditional labour movement. It is a broad democratic alliance of a new kind – an anti-Thatcher alliance – in which the organised working class has a central role but a role which henceforth it will have to *earn* and not *assume*.

A new alliance

In this potentially permanent anti-Thatcher alliance, the women's movement and the peace movement will have prominence because, unlike the bulk of the trade union and labour movement during the run-up to the miners' strike, they have played a crucial role in raising the political consciousness of the British people. It is even conceivable that the churches will have a part in such an alliance because they have raised very pertinent political, social and moral questions during the strike concerning the nature and role of the state and of the dehumanising character of capitalism. In particular, the initiative of the Welsh Council of Churches revealed a very deep understanding of the political origins of the crisis facing all mining regions and put forward proposals to solve them which placed the struggle in the wider context of government energy policy, what they have termed the 'vagaries of an undisciplined free market system' and the need to emphasise the dignity of human beings and communities.

Conscious of the human and organisational forces being unleashed by and for the miners in the midst of the crisis, the Wales Congress in Support of Mining Communities initially set out to bring the debate back to one over the future of the coal industry rather than 'picket line violence' and to increase the unity around the mining communities. It was in effect an all-Wales support group. Its programme of aims highlighted the need to identify and communicate the real issues at stake – the need for a sane energy policy and the safeguarding of jobs, communities, peace and democratic rights. It also sought to encourage local authorities to commission social audits of the effects of the current pit closure programme in their localities (as is being done in other parts of Britain).

At a time when enormous pressures were building up on the NUM in South Wales, particularly as a result of sequestration and fundraising, the Congress sought to get the Welsh people to carry their share of the burden. Indeed, the Congress very quickly received backing from over 300 prominent people in Welsh politics (Plaid, Labour and CP), local government, trade unions, the churches, the arts, farmers, the women's movement and the peace movement. The Congress was born out of a realisation by large sections of the Welsh people that the miners were struggling for the future of Wales. If Thatcherism could defeat the miners, then all Welsh communities were in danger. Its steering committee embraces all these organisations and meets weekly to discuss strategy. As yet there are remarkably few differences over tactics or political initiatives.

The miners' strike has therefore created a Welsh unity and identity, overcoming language and geographical differences, which failed to materialise in 1979 during the devolution referendum when a four to one vote rejected a measure of independence. It was the fear of such a return to the superficial and sterile politics of devolution of 1979 that made a tiny number within the Welsh labour movement hesitate about associating with the Congress. Significantly, their influence was negligible. Dark hints of a 'Commie and Nats plot' was the language of the past. They soon realised that unless they joined, the world would pass them by.

None are minorities
One of the great advantages of the Wales Congress was that it ensured that the NUM, despite serious rebuffs from steelworkers

and lorry drivers, never felt isolated within Wales. For example, just as the Wales Congress was launching a series of nationwide rallies in November, the NCB in South Wales started to increase its aggressive managerial onslaught on the still rock-solid NUM membership. Congress leaders including Labour Euro MP David Morris and Plaid President Dafydd Elis-Thomas MP spearheaded a counterattack by attempting to interview NCB managers personally. They asked why were they, as trade unionists, prepared to supervise scabs (unlike NACODS) and why were they actively participating in a Government plan which would ultimately socially divide and industrially destroy mining communities.

The solidarity of the miners in South Wales held, and the Congress played its part then and later in holding the line to 1 per cent despite over ten months of struggle. After less than two months the Congress was already strengthening itself by decentralisation. There are now local congresses in North Wales, the Rhondda, and the prospect of others in all the Valleys, in London, Ireland and even Nottingham. The strike has therefore not just been about mass picketing. It has been about how people begin to take control of their own lives. It has been about women and men from all the coalfields learning about the many-sided role of the state in industrial battles and that the fight for jobs and communities was and is the experience elsewhere in Britain and abroad. When the South Wales Striking Miners' Choir entertained an entirely black audience in Walsall, one of the choristers paid tribute to the 'ethnic minorities' who had been so outstanding in their support during the strike. A black leader responded: 'The Welsh are the ethnic minority in Walsall.'

The strike has begun to teach us all that none of us are minorities. The Wales Congress is trying to build an anti-Thatcher democratic alliance which will hopefully go beyond the strike and turn all those so-called 'minorities' who have supported us into an irresistible and united majority to fight for peace, jobs and communities. There will inevitably be problems, the greatest of which will be the possibility that all the positive features of unity and experience everywhere could be eclipsed by the fragmentation of the NUM.

5

My Community, My Valley: Onllwyn, Cwm Dulais[*]

A LUNAR OPENCAST LANDSCAPE OF giant cranes and giant lorries: this is the image which comes to mind for visitors who pass through or pass by Onllwyn on their way to waterfalls, country parks, industrial museums or bird gardens. Such visitors would not be aware of a once vibrant community: grazing sheep and recently planted over-green grass have replaced collieries, terraced rows, a school and a chapel. But what of the people? Do we only have a history and what is the essence of that history?

Indeed, the most intriguing irony of the National Eisteddfod arriving in the Neath locality in 1994 was the Onllwyn commemorative plate, with all its scenes from a seemingly long-lost age. The colliery, the school and its main streets of Back and Front Row ('Y Tai') all disappeared in the 1960s and Capel yr Onllwyn finally succumbed in 1992. The original community of Onllwyn now barely exists although its neighbouring

---

[*] First published in Welsh as 'Dysgu trwy Ddwy Iaith ac un Diwylliant: Profiad ac Etifeddiaeth Onllwyn a Chwm Dulais' in Hywel Teifi Edwards (gol./ed.) *Cyfres y Cymoedd: Nedd a Dulais* (Gomer, 1994) and in English as 'Learning through two Languages and one Culture: the Experience of Onllwyn and the Dulais Valley' in *Llafur*, Vol. 6, No. 3, 1994.

communities of Pantyffordd, Dyffryn Cellwen and Banwen all continue to survive and, some would say, thrive. That commemorative plate was one of the reasons why this collection of communities at the head of the Dulais Valley was the first to meet its local funding target for the National Eisteddfod. Why was this?

If we explore this phenomenon, we begin to understand the rootedness and pride in a *Welshness* that is not simply about language and not simply about nostalgia. There is a shared, indeed common inheritance and experience – work, religion, education, politics, popular culture – that can be defined as the unusual lifelong collective learning of this Welsh industrial community between about 1850 and 1960, and that learning has been enriched by the co-existence of the two languages and the diverse origins of our people.

Those of us who caught the end of that time, and still glimpse it now and again, as in 1984–85, bought that commemorative plate with the mixed emotions of nostalgia, anger and inspiration. As all our lives become more privatised in every sense and less rooted in community or collectivist or, dare we say it, proletarian, values, there is still an inner questioning in all of us which is resilient and engaged in valuing the contemporary relevance of some of that time and experience. It is what Gwyn A. Williams, in describing his Dowlais, called 'building a little city of the spirit'.

That is also Onllwyn's inheritance which needs critical understanding and celebrating. But the key word of 'building' implies looking forward to a tangible future whilst recognising the weight and power of a collective memory and a collective history. The *prifardd* Rhydwen Williams captures some of this sense of history in a tribute to a friend, my father Dai Francis, in 1981:

Piau fedd ar y Banwen?
Na, nid oes fedd yma yn un man!
Awelon a gwyntoedd rhydd yr Onllwyn
Fydd ei gofadail ef.

[Does he have a grave at Banwen?
No, there is no grave anywhere!
The breezes and free winds of Onllwyn
Will be his memorial.]

In many ways, Onllwyn has always been at a crossroads. The Romans, as ever, recognised this by locating a strategic fort at neighbouring Coelbren, midway along their Sarn Helen between Swansea and Brecon, and the present-day Roman road, Tonfildre and Maesmarchog are contemporary reminders of this. More recently, in the last century, this was the cultural meeting point of the rural, western, Welsh-speaking anthracite coalfield with its tradition of hunting, shooting, fishing, poaching and farming miners and the largely English-speaking more urban steam coalfield to the east. The booming anthracite collieries of the locality were in every sense a microcosm of the whole coalfield in the inter-war years as they attracted their workforce from every corner of South Wales, and beyond. The distinctive moorland rather than valley landscape, accentuated by what local poet Duncan Bush calls the Montana backdrop of the Cribbarth and the Brecon Beacons, gives the impression of being both worldly and somewhat set apart. The history of our local communities confirms that: fierce local pride expresses itself in the perverse self-deprecating humour of comedian Colin Price in his claim that Banwen was twinned with Beirut, until Beirut protested.

From company town to proletarian community, 1842–1946

A phrase was used in those days, 'people follow the loaf'. The first industrial development in the Dulais Valley was established at Onllwyn by John Williams 'o Fynwy' (from Monmouthshire) who was responsible for creating ultimately what became the centre of the new community: two iron blast furnaces in 1842, two streets of houses ('Y Tai'), the Congregational chapel ('Capel yr Onllwyn') and through his son-in-law, a public house, 'The Onllwyn Inn'.

'Y Tai' remained largely unchanged from their erection in 1848 down to their demolition in 1964. This description by an anthropologist in 1961 is almost timeless:

> The walls are of stone quarried nearby, and roofs are of slates. The floors are of stone flags laid immediately on the ground. Each house has upstairs two bedrooms, and downstairs a small pantry, a very small room which is used mostly as a lumber room and for laying out corpses, and a large living room into which one steps directly from the street. There is neither kitchen nor bathroom, and warm water is provided by a large iron boiler built into the fireplace to the side of the fire. This has to be filled by hand from the cold water tap which has recently been installed … Previously the water was outside in the street. Recently also, electric light has been installed; otherwise there are few labour saving devices. Nearly all domestic duties, including the weekly washing, bathing in a zinc bath, and washing-up have to be performed in the living room which has in addition to the low doorway only one small window which looks out onto the street. Lack of space is worse in Front Row where a small street runs immediately behind and another immediately in front. Inhabitants must cross the street in front to get to their unkept gardens in which are their lavatories and coalsheds …

What they lacked in the comforts of modern living, was compensated for by a strong sense of community. This recollection is of the first decade of the twentieth century:

> … the community was such that everybody trusted each other. In fact no doors were locked at any time of the day. And if anyone

was in need their need would always be supplied by neighbours …
if a cat had kittens everyone knew.

The 1851 census enumerators' books reveal that one-third
of the inhabitants of 'Y Tai' were of Irish origin, and in one
dwelling alone there were as many as sixteen inhabitants. This
young mobile population had all dispersed by 1861, presumably
moving on to Merthyr, Dowlais, Cardiff or America following
the collapse of John Williams' industrial enterprise. The poor
transport links and general geographical isolation meant that
Onllwyn continued to teeter on the brink of reverting to a
marginal farming existence, until the opening of the Neath
and Brecon railway line in 1867 and then the establishing of
Welsh anthracite coal markets in Europe and worldwide from
the 1880s onwards. The neighbouring communities within the
valley, Creunant and Seven Sisters, grew within the local Dulais
Higher Parish, and this most dramatically between 1881 and
1911:

Year	Dulais Higher Parish Population
1801	272
1811	344
1821	362
1831	197
1841	373
1851	824
1861	622
1871	479★
1881	849
1891	1,043
1901	1,806
1911	4,569

★ Census attributes the 1861–71 decline to the 'demolition of blast
furnaces'.

This expansion, of course, mirrors the great growth of the whole of the South Wales coalfield. Onllwyn was a microcosm of this confidently emerging 'American' Wales, sharing the common features of a 'frontier town' and significantly of the community or civic building atmosphere of the time. It was in this key decade of 1901–11 that the individual enterprise represented both by the inrush of single young men seeking work and the paternalist culture of the coal-owners began to be transformed into the collectivist, community and ultimately proletarian culture shaped first by the chapel and then by the local union lodges of the South Wales Miners' Federation, the Fed.

In relative terms, however, it did not, of course, compare with the population explosion of the Rhondda where the social transformation was also more rapid. The Rhondda grew from 951 people in 1851 to 152,781 in 1911. Nonetheless the impact on this small emerging Welsh anthracite community was no less significant. The difference was that all its institutions and workplaces remained predominantly Welsh during this early expansion to such an extent that it was considered to be essentially monoglot Welsh as late as 1907. The question of the language and its inter-relationship with the wider social role of the chapel is key to our understanding of this community at this time.

There is no doubt that this decade of the religious Revival saw the beginning of the high water mark of social influence for the local chapel which extended to the early 1930s, with a fine new building opened in 1909 for the growing congregation embracing over 90 per cent of the local inhabitants. The range of religious, social and cultural activities was crowned by the appointment in 1911 of a 'codwr canu', a choirmaster, Gruffydd Elis Gruffydd (Alawydd Gwyrfil) all the way from Caernarfon. There was growing literacy through the lifelong learning of the chapel's penny readings, Sunday school (thirteen classes by 1913), prayer meetings, a male voice choir, Band of Hope, Rechabites, children's and adults' drama groups, sisterhood and quarterly meetings. A Sunday school outing in 1911 by train to Swansea consisted of five hundred adults and children.

For that generation which grew up in the first three decades of the twentieth century the place of worship was also the place where individual skills of organisation, expression, public speaking and debate as well as collectivist values were all developed and ultimately taken into the new increasingly secular world of the local communities.

By 1914, Onllwyn on the face of it was a 'company' town. Its land, houses, pubs and collieries (with the exception of the oasis of Cwm-Mawr, a haven for the rebel) were all in the hands of the new paternalist Evan Evans-Bevan who had bought out the previous coal-owner, Sir Griffith Thomas. Evans-Bevan seemed to permeate every aspect of this company town, and when that presence was not exerted personally, then his influence was felt through his colliery managers such as Dai 'Baw' Thomas and his colliery officials. Such paternalism was eroded over time with the advent of a more democratic society locally and more widely but at its height it was pervasive and apparently all powerful and never more so than through the medical profession on questions of industrial diseases, injuries and compensation.

But it never quite had the grip on the people of Onllwyn that it did on Seven Sisters, Evans-Bevan's model village, where he built a church, named streets after his children, named the pit and the village after his seven daughters and where he and his family were always feted. By contrast, the impenetrable nature of Welsh Nonconformity, in language, culture and essential democracy, made Onllwyn chapel a counterpoint to the coal-owner, indeed a veritable religious and cultural citadel. Whilst the school and its teachers were important influences on the younger emerging generation, the chapel was, in the words of Dan Lewis, its secretary and later a local headmaster, 'the Official Centre': if Evans-Bevan had the hegemony below ground, it was the chapel which might have had it briefly above ground.

This Welsh rootedness was strengthened in this period through the major influx of population from the west, especially the Swansea Valley. These 'gwŷr ochr draw' were overwhelmingly Welsh in language, Nonconformist in religion and proudly independent in outlook. This autonomy was further helped by the first generation of incomers leaving the company houses of 'Y Tai' and asserting their independence by creating the new community of owner-occupiers at Pantyffordd to the south-west.

By the 1920s, it was still perfectly natural for all community activities, religious and secular, to take place in the chapel, and political awareness might often have been aroused in a Sunday school discussion or a public meeting. The venue for a 'welcome home' for local miners imprisoned following the Ammanford strike of 1925 was the chapel vestry. The skills of choir-master Gruffydd Ellis Gruffydd were put at the disposal of the community fighting for survival in 1926. One child's memory of the time was that he ruined his boy soprano voice through too much penillion singing and concert parties. His repertoire also revealed the increasing anglicisation and cosmopolitan nature of the locality: the Somerset song of 'Oh, No John', 'Macnamara's Band' and 'Nant y mynydd'. That secularisation also manifested itself through the local school with the learning, for example, of the 'Marseillaise' in Welsh.

This anglicisation grew in the inter-war period as the depression to the east meant an in-migration of non-Welsh-speakers from Aberdare, Rhondda, Merthyr and the Monmouthshire valleys. The growing class tensions in the local collieries meant also that the colliery managers and their officials, inevitably influential in the chapels, alienated many miners:

… there was a tendency, say indirectly, for the colliery to have some influence over [chapel] membership because members had a tendency to follow the colliery manager … people followed the loaf … and you couldn't blame them because the collieries in the valley, apart from the Dulais colliery, were owned by the same proprietor … and the local colliery manager was one of the products of the local coal proprietor … there was a pattern [that] someone who was an authority industrially would become a deacon in … the chapel. And their attitude … towards the workmen had a reflection upon the male members of the villages [who ceased to attend].

This class-consciousness expressed itself in unusual and unexpected ways. The coal-owner, 'Mr Bevan', sent the largest wreath to a funeral in 1926. It was met with a mixed response within the family: some were impressed, others thought he could well afford to be generous, given that he paid Samuel Francis, his valued 'vet', only labourer's wages for caring for all his colliery horses in the valley.

This alienation is seared in the memory of Myrddin Powell, still, nearly half a century later:

… [I] always remember this, the manager praying in chapel, and he could pray to God, and the tears were running down … I used to look at him … what a hypocrite I thought. Now the following day, Monday morning then, he was quite the reverse you see. He was a real tyrant of a man … D. J. Thomas … Dai 'Baw' … And in later years, when Hitler came to power, they called him Hitler, and he used to strut around on … the Banwen colliery bank like … Hitler. He used to walk like him.

By the 1930s the wider, more global issues of unemployment, fascism and war placed the miners' union and its political organisations, the Labour Party and the Communist Party, at centre stage, rather than the chapel. Nevertheless, when the

Onllwyn Spanish Aid Committee was set up in 1937, it was chaired by the headmaster, with representatives from every community organisation from the Communist Party to the chapels and the knitting class. This sea change which occurred in the 1930s saw a clear shift away from the chapel (its split was in itself a function of its own crisis of purpose) as the main focus of the community towards the secular world of the union and labour politics. To an extent it was also a language shift as the language of progress and change was perceived universally to be English.

Yet the popularity of Niclas y Glais, the revolutionary poet and Congregational minister, straddled the divide as the community became more proletarianised. The two languages continued to coexist as the new political culture of socialism became so overwhelming that it 'should be weighed not counted in Onllwyn'.

These were the words of D. J. Williams of Tairgwaith, the newly elected MP for Neath, in describing Onllwyn's solidarity: everyone eligible to vote, voted Labour in Onllwyn in 1945.

The commitment to learning, communal values and social justice nurtured in the chapel over time transmuted themselves through secularisation into the labour movement. Pride in the missionary to China, Griffith John, who had once worked in the local colliery in the nineteenth century, and the singing of the imperialistic children's hymn, 'Draw, draw yn China', were from the 1930s onwards seen as the roots which inspired internationalist initiatives. Three local men volunteered for the International Brigades in Spain; the locality provided local platforms for Krishna Menon (India), C. L. R. James (Trinidad) and Cheddi Jagan (Guyana) to speak against British Colonialism long before anti-colonial movements were popular in Britain. All this was a rich mixture of radical, religious and political influences expressed often in both languages.

Whilst the local Sunday school and Band of Hope now had to compete with the Marxist Labour College classes, the Bible could still sit comfortably alongside the crimson rows of the Left Book Club. At the end of 1937 when Dai Francis moved, in one step, from Sunday School teacher to being a member of the Communist Party he could still write in his Bible:

Anrhegwyd hwn i mi gan fy nhad ar ddydd ei ben blwydd 60ain oed, 23ain Rhag 1937. Iachawdwr mawr llenyddol Cymru (Beibl)

[Presented to me by my father on his 60th birthday, 23rd Dec 1937. Great saviour of Welsh literature (The Bible)]

'Gwell yw caru'r ddaear gyfan': Arriving in the new Jerusalem, 1947–64

The nationalisation of the coal industry in 1947 and the creation of the National Health Service in 1948 meant the completion of the journey for one generation and achieved for them a real sense of social justice. The young Communist lodge chairman at Onllwyn, ten years on from inscribing his Bible, addressed the workforce on Vesting Day by quoting Watcyn Wyn's millenarian lines:

Mae teg oleuni blaen y wawr
o wlad i wlad yn dweud yn awr
fod bore ddydd gerllaw.

[Fair light at early dawn
from country to country says now
that break of day is nearby.]

In quoting from his favourite hymn, he was really speaking to his father and his generation who had instilled in him the virtues of chapel attendance, the Welsh language and union membership.

This new world, seemingly a new Jerusalem, was personified in the lives of four local men who worked together for the benefit of the community. John Williams, manager of Onllwyn No. 3 colliery, a lifelong socialist who refused 'to drive men' as a new breed of manager, worked closely with the union and succeeded against the odds in keeping his pit open until 1961. A founder of the Banwen Pony Club, he was active in all spheres of the community, including the bringing of a new progressive doctor, Dafydd Aubrey Thomas, to the locality.

'Doc' was not the patrician of old: a noted actor and lapsed Communist (he left over Lysenko), he brought his friends Ewan McColl, the folk singer, and Hugh McDiarmid the Scottish poet, to Coelbren Club, to perform and drink. He personified the new egalitarianism by his unhesitating solidarity with the miners and the community in which he and his family lived. He described to another friend, the broadcaster Charles Parker, how he was called out to rescue a miner at Onllwyn Colliery in 1961:

… and when I got down there his knee had been bent right back that his tibia and femur were in one straight line and had got thrust straight into the teeth of the coal cutting machine. Now he was doing a job that they call snatching, you see, as they move the cutter up the face, this man's on a rope and he snatches at it to keep the cutter in line with the face when it starts cutting down the face from the gate end. I don't know how it happened, but he'd probably stumbled or something, and tripped forward and his knee got caught or bent up under him and got pulled into the cutter. Well I went down there, and there was this chap stuck fast in the cutter, the cutter stopped, but you could really see his knee through the far end, the operational end of the cutter, and we had a short pow-wow as to how we were going to get him out of it, and he was perfectly calm, perfectly collected in terrible pain, very wan looking, very pale, but all he was concerned about was just waiting until we could get started on the job. Well the gate end was pretty rickety on top, you know, and bits were coming down through, and posts were all sort of feeling the squeeze at the top, and so we decided to put a hand sylvester on the cutter and try and reverse it very slowly back by hand to ease his leg out. So I got down underneath him now, and I was sitting there with him in my lap and my hands right forward into the cutter, trying to make sure that when they did reverse it by hand, on the sylvester, that the teeth of the cutter would go back into the same holes and not chew his leg up any more. So we eased him back gently into exactly the same holes they'd taken up on the way in and do his leg less damage. Well, what one's impressed with in a scene like that is just the readiness of help, you know the roof's all falling in, and you have to stay the cutter against the posts keeping the top up, to stop it shifting when it takes the strain from the sylvester, and although the posts keep knocking out you had an embarrassment of help, and it really makes you realise what grand guys these people are, they just are the salt of the earth, no danger keeps them away from an injured man, and when posts all begin to shift they're all in the middle of it putting new ones up, it doesn't matter what risk it is to them, or to anybody, but the only person that matters is the patient; and it sort of epitomises this Hippocratic thing in medicine that what matters is the patient, and they all have the same sort of feeling, it's a sort of *esprit de corps* that you get underground, you never meet with it anywhere else, I've never met with it anywhere else in the world …

Of course the amazing thing about it is that the very next morning in cold blood, they go back into a place where the same thing can well happen, well they're not sort of keyed to it by the knowledge that it will, but are dogged by the knowledge that it might all the time; and it's this cold-blooded heroism that you get among miners, that they've got a sort of calm philosophic acceptance of the unusual, because it happens very frequently and yet it isn't usual, so that they are not keyed to it in the sense of a man going over the top in a battle or anything like that, he's keyed to it, he's led out to it perhaps with, or without, a glass of rum or whatever the hell they give them to go over the top. But these people go down after a cold breakfast early in the morning in the winter, to the same set of circumstances, where the same thing can happen any second, and they just go on with it as just a day's job, a day's work. That's the unusual thing to me …

There was also Vivian Jones, the last full-time minister at Onllwyn, who came as a young man to the village, enthused a younger generation with a social gospel (as Erastus Jones did in neighbouring Seven Sisters) and borrowed the *Communist Manifesto* to better understand Onllwyn. In his funeral tribute in 1972 to the agnostic Dr Thomas he pleasantly surprised the chapel congregation by saying that in their long discussions, they realised that they shared the same religion, it was 'honest doubt'.

And there was Dai Francis, later general secretary of the Miners' Union in South Wales, founding chair of TUC Cymru and member of the Gorsedd as 'Dai o'r Onllwyn'. In presiding over the opening of the Onllwyn Miners' Welfare Hall in July 1955, he helped complete the secular revolution which had commenced in the 1930s: with its range of social, cultural, political and sporting activities, the hall finally eclipsed the chapel as the centre of the village.

Yet, that chapel ethos permeated the hall, through its Welshness, its puritanism, its *grân,* its community focus. And yet, too, as if to reaffirm a regression into an even more male culture, the hall was less egalitarian than the chapel where women always played a significant and ultimately dominant role: at its closure in 1992 a majority of the deacons were women and its *mixed* choir in 1951 won first prize at the South Wales Miners' Eisteddfod, a feat never to be achieved by the still all-*male* choir based at the hall.

Much more important than this secularisation in effecting changing gender roles was the other local event in July 1955: the opening of the pit-head baths which belatedly liberated women more than men. It was in part a recognition of this sexual revolution, and also respect, indeed deference, towards local educational achievement, that Dr Phylis (Colenso) Jones, who had been born in 'Y Tai', was invited to perform the opening of the Onllwyn Welfare Hall. There was a certain poetic justice in the two buildings opening almost simultaneously.

That confident world, full of hope for the future, came to an abrupt halt with the closure of Onllwyn No. 1, the last colliery in the northern end of the valley. That closure in 1964 coincided with the only time its new banner was carried at the South Wales Miners' Gala bearing a version of Elfed's internationalist line, 'Gwell yw Caru'r Ddaear Gyfan' / 'It is Better to Love the Whole World'. Typically, the banner was laid to rest in a Soviet mining museum in the Ukraine, a full generation before the Dulais Valley was to have its own museum.

A community without a colliery, from 1964

> … the local culture is changing perceptibly. It is constantly under attack and in the National Coal Board's long-term plan for the coalfield lies a threat to the survival of the culture and even of the community itself.

This pessimistic prediction in the early 1960s was all the more difficult to accept, given the relative and uninterrupted prosperity under private and public ownership. The Dulais Valley under early nationalisation had indeed been unusual in many ways. Its wages were 8 per cent higher than the rest of the anthracite coalfield and 14 per cent higher than the rest of the whole coalfield in 1935. Remarkably it had more work than people, with 1,500 men still travelling into the valley as late as 1958. The paternalism had also lasted longer: the essentially family firm of Evans-Bevan was somewhat unique in the coalfield in that it had survived amalgamations down to 1947.

That sense of stability and optimism changed to pathos and anger over time and can be traced in Welsh through local poets

Gwilym Bugail (Gwilym Davies) and Ben Dulais (Ben Davies) and in English in the 1940s by B. L. Coombes (of Resolven and Banwen), in the 1950s and 1960s by Menna Gallie (of Ystradgynlais and Creunant), and in the 1970s by Brian Morgan Francis (of Pantyffordd). By the 1980s we have the anguish of Duncan Bush (of Ynyswen) whose 'Summer 1984' emphasised the continuity of family, communal and class solidarity. His descriptions of the local valleys in the epic strike of 1984–85 are principally of Onllwyn Welfare Hall, the true epicentre of the struggle:

> in workmen's clubs and miners' welfare
> halls, just as it had been once, communities
> beleaguered but the closer,
>
> the interest for it, with resources
> now distributed to need, and organised to last,
> the dance floors stacked
>
> with foodstuffs like a dockside, as if
> an atavistic common memory, an inheritance
> perhaps long thought romantic
>
> like the old men's proud and bitter
> tales of 1926 ...

And as if to pay singular tribute, his other poem in the same collection, 'Onllwyn, West Glamorgan, 1985', conveys precisely the haunting angry emotions of the time.

There is something baffling about the survival of a village without its pit; none more so than Onllwyn. It was as if people associated with it (but who have long moved on) wanted to recapture a special moment in time. And that moment in time came again when the Welfare Hall was the centre for three valleys in 1984–85: its support group, its women's group, its weekly newspaper *The Valleys' Star,* the strike committee, the food distribution for a thousand families and the South Wales striking miners' choir. Its secretary Alun Thomas (known locally as 'our foreign secretary' because of his long absences) was the coalfield's most effective campaigner and fundraiser in Ireland, North Wales, London and secretly even in Nottingham, establishing a range of remarkable links including uniquely with the Gays and Lesbians Miners' Support Group.

Long after Blaenant (the last colliery in the valley) closed in 1990, the political inheritance endures, personified in Alun Thomas and many others, who were elected to positions of responsibility in local government. Equally significant was the emergence of women in public life. Moira Lewis, again prominent in the YMCA in the 1950s and the Welfare Hall in the 1960s and in local government from the 1980s, allied herself with a new generation of women who emerged in 1984–85. Forming a women's training centre, DOVE at Banwen, they provide new educational opportunities for local women, networking locally and throughout Europe with other educational groups committed to progress through community development. It was this inspirational initiative which ultimately gave birth to the concept of the Community University of the Valleys in a three-way partnership between Onllwyn Community Council, DOVE and University College Swansea in 1993.

In an age without coal, this once again increasingly bilingual learning culture can fulfil personal and collective dreams at the end of a century of local endeavour illustrated by that commemorative plate.

6

My Club:
'Magnificent Seven'*

W HEN SEVEN SISTERS PLAYED the postponed Welsh Rugby Union Cup game against Pontypridd in December 1976 the occasion was redolent with personal memories. My late father Dai Francis, a keen supporter and long-standing patron of the club, who had moved from the valley over a quarter of a century before, wanted to 'place' every player and every replacement within the families he had known in his youth. Names like Howell, Best, Bowen and Scully were easy. Thomas, Lewis, James, Price, Williams, Evans, Llewellyn and Morgan obviously proved a little more difficult. As I recall I think he only failed with one: Dai John who in marrying Gwyneth had moved to Seven Sisters in the last decade. 'Jack Best, John's grandfather, was a solid trade unionist: always paid his dues first. He came from Dowlais, where there was a lot of victimisation,' was a typical recollection.

And then more recently in its centenary year there were three funerals which connected us personally with every decade of the club's first century, and a birth which connected us with the next century.

---

* First published in my *Magnificent Seven 1897–1997: The Centenary History of Seven Sisters Rugby Football Club* (Gwasg Morgannwg, 1997).

In 1996–97 we lost three distinguished and valued members. There was W. E. ('Wep') Price, player, committee man and a life-member whose extended family included many players for the club and whose father, according to legend, scored the first try for Seven Sisters. And then there was Brian James, one of our brightest stars of the 1960s and 1970s whose try against Vardre from his own line is still remembered with awe and disbelief today: his wicked smile, unorthodox darting runs and quick wit lives on with us all. In the changing room before a game in 1973 there was much leg-pulling of Dennis Williams about his 'qualifying' to play for the neighbouring county of Breconshire. Brian had the answer: Dennis' mother bought eggs in Brecon market.

And finally, there was Phil 'Bach' Davies, buried in Creunant, but six bearers were from the Seven Sisters club. 'Why?' asked the vicar. The first answer was swept away by the wind, and just as well. The complex truth was that Phil Bach, one of the most talented players to be produced by Seven Sisters, belonged to the whole valley. He had played for Seven Sisters as early as 1928–29, along with his three brothers Rees, Tom and Jack, and later for Creunant and Swansea and rugby league for Rochdale Hornets. His remains were to be in Creunant where he had spent the last years of his life with Mairwen, his wife. But his talented sons, Philip, Beverley (a Secondary Schools cap who played for Neath, Llanelli and Nice) and Lance (a Neath player and like his father a rugby league star, with Bradford Northern) had all, along with their father, learnt much of their rugby at Seven Sisters, were proud of that and wished to acknowledge that. Moelwyn Evans, a long-standing Seven Sisters player, could now reveal, with the professionalising of the game, that he had the unique distinction of playing with all three sons and the father (on his return from Rochdale Hornets he played under an assumed name at Maesteg for Seven Sisters). And so the sharing of his funeral in this way explained everything.

Then there was the birth of Ifan, son of Dathyl and Carwyn and grandson of Ann and Moelwyn, nephew of the current player Hywel. In his own inimicable way, Moelwyn proclaims that Carwyn will be the fourth generation of the family to play for Seven Sisters, even though his father, uncles and other grandfather are past and present Ystradgynlais players. Ifan's brother or sister yet to be born may perhaps play for Ystradgynlais. Anything is possible.

It is evident from these recollections that our history is important to us. The first hundred years of rugby football at Seven Sisters is more than just the story of the game itself, played by young men on a Saturday afternoon. It is the story not only of a voluntary sporting organisation but of its changing community in the first century of its life. That is why the game, as a mirror of that community, evokes and provokes such strong arguments, sometimes quarrels, much passion, fierce loyalty and most of all, fellowship and comradeship: in many ways to understand the club we must understand the community and its families upon which it depended.

D. J. Davies (Dai Tim), one of the most remarkable servants of the club, stood down as its secretary in 1971. He recalled then with pride that Seven Sisters 'was one of the best-known clubs in Welsh rugby, a club known, respected and envied, feared and hated on the field'. His words and actions were always colourful and were a bright emblem of all those who selflessly sacrificed time and energy off the field to make the game possible in the village, despite feeling like 'a wet echo' after working nights at the local colliery and being 'an incorrigible worrier' about his club's future.

It is for these reasons, our collective pride in our collective past and a recognition of the sacrifices of the countless numbers whose voluntary efforts have allowed Seven Sisters RFC to prosper, that I dedicated the history to the women and men who laboured and continue to labour, off the field to support 'Magnificent Seven'.

The history of rugby football in Seven Sisters mirrors the history of the village itself: struggling to emerge in the early decades, growing into maturity and success in mid-century and consolidating its pre-eminence as one of the best clubs in Wales as it approached its centenary. And all this was achieved despite considerable changes in its economic fortunes particularly in the last three decades of its first century.

Seven Sisters was, and many would say still is, a typical South Wales Valleys community. It was created in the last great surge of the Industrial Revolution with the vast expansion of the South Wales coalfield in the last quarter of the nineteenth century. Located in the Dulais Valley within the western anthracite coalfield, between the neighbouring communities of Creunant to the south and Onllwyn and Banwen to the north-east, it took its name from the pit which was sunk by the local coal-owner Evan Evans-Bevan between 1872 and 1875, and for several years the community was known simply as 'Seven Sisters Colliery': colliery and community were synonymous, work and place were intertwined then and for decades later.

Evan Evans-Bevan was typical of the South Wales coal-owners of the time. He owned most of the collieries of the valley, its land, most of its houses, pubs and the Vale of Neath brewery at Cadoxton. Some felt he owned the people. He was nonetheless a benefactor and a patriarch and felt Seven Sisters of all the communities in the valley was 'his' village. He named the colliery after his seven daughters and in turn the village took its name from the colliery. He built St Mary's Church in 1911 and the *Kelly's Directory of Monmouthshire and South Wales* in 1895 and 1920 faithfully record the rapid change from a small, essentially rural settlement (with echoes of an American coal camp) to a substantial industrial community:

St Mary's mission church at Seven Sisters, a building of iron, will seat 200 persons; Rev. Owen Davies of St Aidan's, has been curate in charge since 1894. There are chapels for Baptists, Welsh Calvinistic Methodists, Congregationalists and Wesleyans.

Here are several anthracite collieries. Sir John Talbot Dillwyn Llewellyn Bart is Lord of the Manor and principal land owner. The soil is clay, sub-soil blue clay, and the land is chiefly pasture. The area is 6,261 acres, rateable value £6832 and the population (of Dylais Higher Parish Church which included part of Creunant as well as Onllwyn and Banwen) in 1891 was 1043. [1895]

The church of St Mary, locally in Seven Sisters and erected in 1911 at a cost of £6000, the gift of E. Evans–Bevan esq., is a building of stone in the Early English style and consists of chancel, nave, north and south aisles and a bell turret. The organ which cost £600, was also the gift of E. Evans–Bevan esq.: there are 476 sittings … The living is a vicarage, net yearly value £352 in the gift of E. Evans–Bevan … The population assigned to the district (Dylais Higher) was 4851. [1920]

It was within this rapidly expanding confident society which saw population grow nearly five-fold in a quarter of a century that rugby football began in Seven Sisters in 1897.

Whilst the coal-owner was often dominant and influential he was not all powerful. Evans–Bevan did become the rugby club's first president but there were other influences and other centres of power, for as anyone who has ventured to Seven Sisters will testify, the community is complex with a myriad of family, social, sporting, cultural and religious organisations as well as many small businesses. Local and family loyalties counted and still count for a great deal.

By the early decades of the century the community could boast branches of Barclays and Lloyds Banks, two schools (built in 1883 and 1897), a local doctor (Christopher Armstrong, MB BCh, 'physician and surgeon'), a reading room, a brass band (formed in

1886) and a wide range of local shopkeepers and farmers including David Aaron (draper), Mrs Lizzie Bowden (bootmaker), William Davies (dairymen), Daniel Evans (Brynteg farm), John Francis George (ironmonger), David R. Harris (Seven Sisters Inn), Rhys Harris (stationer), Thomas Harris (chemist), David Thomas Levi (Bryndulais Inn), William Morgan (butcher), William Morgan (farm bailiff to Evans-Bevan), Howell Powell (fried fish dealer), George Price (baker), Evan Thomas (builders) and William Thomas (hairdresser).

For all its complexity, Seven Sisters was and still is a working-class community, but of a particular distinctive kind. It may have what one observer in the 1970s called a sprinkling of 'thirty bob snobs' but these are hard to find today and would certainly never be found in Seven Sisters Rugby Club.

Its distinctiveness is in its enduring attachment to that semi-rural bilingual anthracite world of close-knit communities with a fierce pride in family and local connections. In the summer of 1972 I turned up for a trial. Having lived away from the Valley for over a decade I was politely quizzed by Emyr Lewis, the club secretary: 'Were you born in Seven? Have you moved to Seven? Have you married a Seven girl?' The answers were not that hopeful: I had moved to Ystradgynlais (an 'ochr draw'), Mair, my wife had been born in Barry (almost England) but I could claim to have been born in neighbouring Onllwyn and one uncle and several cousins (at least five) had played for the club. 'Bring your kit on Tuesday, we'll have a look at you,' was his noncommittal reply. Tuesday came, the connections had been checked and there was the usual warm welcome, but it was only what was to be expected. Twenty years later my son was asked why he played for the youth side, when he lived in a neighbouring village. 'Tradition' was the swift and unhesitating reply.

The rugby club came into existence in 1897 as one of the

many collectivist democratic organisations emerging at the time across all the Valleys of South Wales – chapels, brass bands, co-operative societies, friendly societies, trade union lodges, sporting organisations. They were all in their different ways confident expressions of a booming if unequal society. One miners' union across the whole coalfield was not achieved until 1898, the eight-hour day was not won until 1908, the minimum wage not until 1912, men were killed frequently, often through negligence of coal-owners with 439 being sacrificed in Senghennydd in 1913, and women lived difficult lives themselves, with more dying in childbirth in such places as the Rhondda than miners killed underground at the turn of the century.

These were turbulent times, the Valleys being described as an 'American' Wales. The religious Revival of 1904–5 gripped many in Seven Sisters as elsewhere, with Salem, Seion and Soar being built in quick succession. The Liberal cabinet minister Lloyd George came into the Valleys, indeed to Seven Sisters, to quell the rising tide of industrial unrest and socialist thinking. Seven Sisters won a reputation as one of the most militant, most socialist, most internationalist lodges in the coalfield. In the 1940s it was one of the centres of the unofficial boys' strikes and its lodge banner in the 1950s proudly proclaimed under Picasso's dove of peace 'y byd yn un mewn heddwch' (the world as one in peace).

At a time when children left school at eleven or twelve years of age, and many born before 1870 had little or no schooling at all, the people of Seven Sisters as elsewhere learnt quickly through their work and life experiences. Education was not free and compulsory until 1891, and by 1912 boys passing a 'labour exam' were deemed to be sufficiently educated to leave school and enter the man's world of the colliery. The organisations which the community created in the crucially formative years before the Great War reflected the adversity of the time, the working-class nature of the community, the growing solidarity below ground and the patriarchal dominance in public life, especially the pit, the union, the chapel, the pub the institute/reading room, the co-op, the band and finally, when it came in 1897, the rugby club.

Such organisations were informal schools of learning for adults, providing different forms of spiritual and material sustenance. Rugby football was part of the learning process, introducing boys to a man's world, inducting them into the world of comradeship, fellowship and in the words of Morris Davies, the long-standing club chairman from the 1970s to the 1980s, the importance of being good citizens. And part of that, of course, was the need to learn about a sense of 'chwarae teg' (fair play) – presumably as opposed to rough play? This concept was redolent with the universal working-class aspiration of social justice which often made referees slightly suspect in Seven Sisters. 'Chwarae yw'r wobr' (playing is the prize) appears on the Seven Sisters club badge but winning through fair play was also a keen aspiration for 'Magnificent Seven': its history and its community have always made that an imperative.

And as if to emphasise this very special place in the wider cultural and political life of Wales its ladies' team (whose formation I had predicted in the original centenary history in 1997) is a sparkling example of the transformation of a previously male dominated society. A valley which was part of the solidarity link with the gay community during the miners' strike of 1984–85 (and celebrated in the film *Pride*) now today, a generation later, boasts a gay icon in Bethan Kelland-Howell as the founder not only of its ladies' team, but also an Ospreys and Welsh international player. Solidarity has a particular meaning here.

7

Communities, Universities and a New Beginning*

PRIFYSGOL Y WERIN – the People's University – is an idea which has both inspired and confused us. Raymond Williams once wrote sceptically of the word 'community' because its definition was elusive. And so it is with Prifysgol y Werin, so long the description of the organic relationship between the University of Wales, its colleges and the people of Wales. It is time for us to look again at its true origins, how it has influenced us and how to re-define it more clearly for the twenty-first century: a place of excellence that is not elitist, a place of higher learning serving more diverse needs and diverse expectations and, most critically of all, in a democratic partnership with the wider community. Jan Hulley, one of the adult students on the Community University of the Valleys, described it challengingly as 'a community of learning'. Hywel Ceri Jones of the European Commission again recently spoke of 'anchoring the University ... in the communities of the Valleys'. Both images are good starting points.

The idea that universities have that wider community role grew out of the Enlightenment and gathered pace in the latter part of the nineteenth century. University Extension, as it became

---

* First published as 'Do Miners Read Dickens? Communities, Universities and a New Beginning' in *The Welsh Journal of Education*, Vol. 6, No. 1, 1997.

known, took many forms in different times and in different countries. In Britain, for the most part, it became known as the 'liberal' tradition – 'Y gwaith traddodiadol' (the traditional work) with the creation of extra-mural departments in virtually every university by the 1920s.

Elsewhere this liberal ethos took the form of the Land-Grant and Sea-Grant Universities of the Mid and Far West of the United States in the nineteenth century and the Popular University of Italy in the early twentieth century which was much criticised by the Italian Marxist, Antonio Gramsci, for its inferior curriculum and its condescension. This interface of 'community' and 'higher education', especially in times of crisis, has never been straightforward, and never more so than today.

As an aside, to confuse matters a little further, I am reminded of my own experience: two young lecturers, Peter Stead and Neil Harding, speaking during a students' occupation at Swansea in 1969, on 'Socialism' and 'Syndicalism' respectively. And later, in 1974, I addressed a students' occupation in the University College Swansea Registry on the 'Origins of Workmen's Institutes'. This is to hint at a more complex world where education's social role can be questioning, indeed subversive of received wisdom. By contrast, the 'liberal tradition' could have a darker side to it which was more to do with crude 'social engineering' and social control. Let us look at the Welsh experience to explore that complexity.

The Welsh experience

The first historians of the University of Wales wrote of it as 'the creation not of sovereigns and statesmen, but of the people themselves', that enduring belief in its popular origins. This has also been explored by the official history in which Professor J. Gwynn Williams puts everyone in their place. Whilst the university was not strictly speaking built with 'the pennies of the poor', they did however give 'a great deal more than might reasonably have been expected of them, industrialists and landowners a great deal less in proportion to their resources.'

But that wider role has never been a simple one. As Wales expanded in population at the beginning of the century, it became more cosmopolitan, more secular, more anglicised, more proletarianised, and as a consequence more awkward. The liberal, 'missionary', idea of a community of interests began to break down. The newly emerging ruling elites of Welsh society began to worry particularly about these awkward coalfield communities in the South Wales Valleys and elsewhere, particularly as they had their own ideas about education as an emancipating force. They were creating their own organic intellectuals.

Principal Reginald Montagu Burrows of King's College London in a moment of clarity, for which historians are eternally grateful, spoke of the real purpose of the 'missionary type work' of the University Settlements. His speech was reported in *The Welsh Outlook*, what could be described as the internal bulletin of the emerging Welsh Establishment:

> The vast majority of working men, whatever their political and industrial views, have the national characteristics of moderation and common-sense, love of order and piety … They fully recognise the priceless contribution which the richer classes can and shall bring towards the remoulding of that new and greater Britain. Apart from all snobbery, they genuinely admire the qualities of the 'gentleman' in the sense in which you would like your sons to understand the word … It is in this spirit that we ask Cardiff and South Wales to approach the Settlement Movement. That way lies Evolution. Is it to be that or Revolution? Which will you have? [January 1914]

Two years later, in the midst of the Great War in which the miners of South Wales defeated the Liberal Government in an industrial battle, *The Welsh Outlook* grappled with the problem:

To the average Britisher, the Welsh miner is an enigma ... South Wales is the industrial storm centre of Great Britain. The Welsh miner is always in the van of Trade Union progress; what he suggests today, his comrades in other coalfields adopt tomorrow. It must however surely be obvious in view of the important results which may accrue from wrong systems of education both to the mining community and the nation at large, that the subject of civil, economic and political education should be carefully considered with a view to the provision of some State-aided system on unbiased lines, which will appeal to the largest possible number of young men residing in our teeming mining valleys. [July 1916]

And then proposed a solution, a month later, entitled 'The University's Opportunity':

Here lies ample scope for a real live University, or University College. Hitherto, university education in South Wales has been for the few; what is wanted is a University with a missionary spirit that will spread its teaching to the Valleys of the coalfield and will equip minds, now immature, to deal with the great problems that vitally affect the social life of the nation. [August 1916]

Such concerns were constantly expressed, not always publicly, down to the 1930s, and certainly informed public policy throughout Britain, most noticeably the famous 1919 report of the Adult Education Committee of the Ministry of Reconstruction, out of which grew university extension movements throughout Britain.

University College Swansea in its early years was created in an atmosphere of 'underlying anxiety to counter the militant influence of the Central Labour College, and the growth of "syndicalism" in industrial South Wales'. The rise of what became known as Marxist independent working-class education, particularly out of such trade unions as the South Wales Miners' Federation, was a major feature of politics and adult education in this period. It was with some relief that the Carnegie-funded Joint Committee for the Promotion of Educational Facilities in the South Wales and Monmouthshire Coalfield could at last report in 1929:

> It seemed at one time that the miner in South Wales was going to replace the old native culture with another – a culture based on his needs as worker and fostered by means of the classes of the National Council of Labour Colleges. This period has definitely passed … He is now groping back towards his old anchorages and is taking a new interest in Music, in Literature, in Psychology, and in particular in Religion – not necessarily the orthodox religion in creeds, but his religion as expressing the philosophy of life.

Thankfully, that essentially patriarchal and hierarchical view and essentially from outside, was never dominant: it was not the full story nor the end of the story. On the contrary, the colleges of the University of Wales have always acknowledged that they have grown out of a democratic tradition and are very much rooted in that tradition, even if sometimes, as with Iolo Morganwg, we have helped to invent the tradition. Whilst it is important to acknowledge that our Continuing Education departments emerged as a consequence of the very real social and political tensions in our society, they were also influenced in a positive way by them.

As if to emphasise the complementary nature of two traditions it is no accident that Professor Glanmor Williams could truthfully say on the occasion of the opening of the South Wales Miners' Library in October 1973 that bringing together the university and the Miners' Union was a modern version of that democratic partnership between the university and the people, Prifysgol y Werin, the People's University.

Indeed, to use the language of today, it has always been acknowledged that a 'learning society' is dependent on 'wealth creation'. The most successful period for these twin aspirations in recent Welsh history was the half-century from 1870 to 1920, precisely the time of the emergence of the University of Wales and the growth in adult learning expectations beyond the university, most notably the miners' institutes and their libraries throughout the Valleys. These institutes and libraries were but one aspect of modern Welsh popular formal and informal learning within which university adult education has been located, not separate and apart but integral to it: in many ways they were part of that growing literate society upon which the university could build its early foundations.

Voices of learning

Time and time again historians have been struck by the diversity of that collective lifelong learning of the coalfield. Josiah Jones (Joe Brickman), a founder of the Cwmllynfell Miners' Welfare Association and a member of Saunders Lewis' and Hywel Teifi Edwards' Welsh literature classes, began his own self-education in the Sunday school, where children and adults learnt together: he ended his days attending my classes in the late 1970s:

> ... Oedd dylanwad y capel yn gryfach amser 'na [1900], pan oe'n ni'n blant ... a oedd 'i Gymraeg e'n fantais fawr. Na le oedd pobol a plant ... yn dod i ddarllen Cymraeg.

> *[... The influence of the chapel was greater at this time [1900] when I was a child ... and its Welsh was of great advantage. It was here that adults and children learnt to read Welsh.]*

This growing learning environment also became a reason for in-migration. John Williams left rural Merionethshire in 1906 for the expanding cosmopolitan 'American Wales' of the South Wales coalfield because of the educational opportunities. The contrast was striking:

School … was three miles from home … I attended … for five years nominally but within that time it didn't amount to more than two years because of the gaps. Bad weather, long distance, and the demands for child labour on the small farms in our district … my imagination I suppose had been fired more or less by some of the advantages of going to South Wales … and I thought there would be an opportunity for more self-education in mining villages and that proved to be true.

What I have been describing is very much a nineteenth-century collective working-class 'self-help' phenomenon, an early form of autonomous and often collective lifelong learning, the extent of which is still difficult to conceive for the 'outsider' looking back to another time and another world. Take, for example, the two professors looking upwards at a shelf-ful of the collected works of Charles Dickens and one asking the question, 'Do miners read Dickens?' I was eavesdropping on the conversation: it was 1983. As an oral historian and an adult education tutor, I thought it was an interesting piece of historical evidence and cultural alienation to be stored up for future use.

We were standing in the South Wales Miners' Library at University College Swansea: the library had been created as a result of a major SSRC project which rescued the collections of remarkable books from workmen's institutes – what one historian, Professor Dai Smith, frequently called the brains of the coalfield.

The question however was a serious one, for it did raise some important further cultural questions about the history and nature of adult education in Wales and the complex relationship of the university to the wider community. Have we seen ourselves as missionaries or as visionaries? How has our mission or our vision changed over time, for Wales inhabits a very different material world now? The miners and their industry have largely gone, but the people and the communities remain and their collectivist vision remains strong as evidenced by the successful Tower Colliery workers' buy-out. How has the idea of lifelong learning changed in this century? Can we legitimately talk of what I have called already 'collective lifelong learning' – the way in which we learn from one another individually and collectively, in communities, in the work place, in social movements and in universities, throughout the whole of our lives, as citizens rather than as customers?

The cornerstone of these adult learning initiatives was the institutes and libraries. Tredegar had by 1951 over 23,000 books, two branch libraries, a reading machine for the blind, a picture library, film club, cinema, a brass band, operatic society, drama groups, evening classes, snooker tables, lectures by poets such as Masefield and politicians of the standing of MacDonald and Snowden. It was for good reason that Tredegar's most famous son, Aneurin Bevan, would say that his education began the day he left school with the acquiring of a borrower's ticket for the institute library.

Even in the depths of the Depression, Cwmaman's Institute in the Cynon Valley could boast two halls, a library, gymnasium, billiard hall, band room and twenty local societies from rifle clubs to study circles. And then there was Gregorio Esteban conducting informal Spanish classes through the medium of Welsh on a Saturday night at Abercraf Miners' Welfare Hall.

What we have been exploring is the role of adult education, even in the most difficult and abject times, being seen as a resource for enlightenment and for changing circumstances, individually and collectively, creating social spaces for working people. Take the example of the future miners' leader Will Paynter who retreated into reading after the defeat of 1926, and Mavis Llewellyn who believed that the miners' defeat of 1926 led to families deciding education should be seen as a ladder outwards.

And as that process of 'learning' is at the heart of the personal journey from surviving to living we see three generations of self-taught men and women, organic intellectuals, hundreds indeed thousands of them, who had a universal vision. The writer Gwyn Thomas talks about one of them in *The Colliers' Crusade*, which traced the political education of those men who went off to fight fascism in the Spanish Civil War:

> Lewis Jones, a man of rare ability, novelist, orator … one of the great interpreters of the modern spirit … In the concentration of his passionate devotion to the idea of change through thought he was saintly.

Learning from our inheritance

What relevance does all this have for us in the universities of today? Edward Said has written of the way in which the past invades the present: 'Appeals to the past are among the commonest of strategies in interpretations of the present.' In the contest over cultural territory the discussions about what is taught, how it is taught, where it is taught and who is taught are fundamental. Said again, quoting Basil Davidson, gives us some clues as to how we should respond to rapid and devastating social change:

> … there comes the period … when efforts are made to reconstitute a 'shattered' community, to save or restore the sense and fact of community …

That recognition of shared collective values cannot be underestimated. There is no doubt that giving 'historical depth' to educational strategies of the present is both valid and vital. The rootedness of our university in our communities, in our region, in our country Wales, increasingly in the wider European context, and its responsiveness and accessibility to all, is imperative.

That rootedness is exemplified in the small town of Briton Ferry, radical, dissenting, socialist. Its extra-mural classes nurtured by such illustrious adult tutors as the one-time barber, the late Bill Gregory, and my friend and formerly my colleague, Tom Thomas. That town boasted the largest Independent Labour Party (ILP) branch in Britain and the greatest concentration of conscientious objectors in the First World War. It attracted, as a matter of course, the Russian/American anarchist Emma Goldman and the Trinidadian writer C. L. R. James. Classes in such places were inevitably woven into the local popular political culture. James may have completed his masterpiece *Black Jacobins* in 1938 while staying in Creunant in the Dulais Valley because of the quality of Brinley Griffiths' library, a local headmaster and part-time adult educator.

The university extra-mural class at Briton Ferry was very much part of that local culture: as rooted as the Co-operative Society, the Workers' Educational Association and the ILP Library. We can also trace such connections through chapels, 'The White House' and the 'Pick and Shovel' Social Club into the WEA and our classes in the Ammanford of the 1980s.

The university into the community: a new beginning?

This 'connectedness' with communities has been our inheritance. Recent innovative developments have merely built on these community-based foundations of learning. One such initiative is the Community University of the Valleys: the idea of student negotiated, locally-based, student-centred self-contained higher education learning opportunities. The fact that the Community University of the Valleys owed its existence to a coalition of diverse social partners – a women's group (DOVE), local authorities, the university, the European Commission, Higher Education Funding Council (Wales) – converging during and after the miners' strike of 1984–85 is also not a new phenomenon. That the university can and did make an intervention at a time of community crisis is nevertheless important.

Its intervention in providing community guidance for redundant miners and in taking the lead in the creation of the Valleys' Initiative for Adult Education was a notion of solidarity that was also critical. But the emphasis was always on a social and democratic partnership rather than missionary work. The real lead was taken not by the university but by women who identified their own autonomous needs and saw the importance of building democratic networks as they had in 1984–85. A video made of the women's experiences of the time was produced by one of our extra-mural classes. It emphasised the collective learning of women which led to the creation in 1985 of the DOVE workshop, a women's educational and training initiative, and which ultimately led to the Community University of the Valleys in 1993. Wendy Headon, active during 1984–85, and later a student at the Community University, is living testimony of the organic link between informal and formal learning and the essential social movements of the wider community.

Our experience with the Community University gives us some clues for the future. It raises questions about the nature and role of a university. It should not necessarily however be seen as a new beginning but more the past invading the present, and there are many reasons for saying this. Firstly, the modernising of the idea of a 'People's University' means the development of democratic and strategic partnerships which will result in the university becoming more of an integral part of the local community. A clearer and more coherent regional strategy by the university, taking account of the changing local educational and industrial scene, is the kind of model recognised by the European Union, relying more on cooperation than on competition, as with such Motor Regions as Catalonia. The extent to which the university takes account of the pivotal role of further education and the way it assists regional industrial and social regeneration through research and graduate studies, particularly with small and medium sized private and public enterprises, will be a measure of that integration.

Secondly, the idea of such a 'People's University' means greater and wider accessibility for sections of local society which have hitherto been under-represented in higher education. Barriers of social class, gender, ethnic origin, disability and age are gradually being removed here at Swansea as elsewhere. Equal opportunities strategies will be accelerated through the growth of part-time, flexible study and student-centred learning which recognise the diversity of students' needs and aspirations. Already over half the students in British higher education are mature age and part-time. This change also extends to location: students may be campus based, work based or community based. Accrediting chunks of learning throughout life as and when needed with guidance, crèche, open and distance learning support, should be the key ingredients for all further and higher education. But again this would not be a new beginning: as we have seen, our communities have always striven for such lifelong educational opportunities but have only glimpsed them in the past. The shift towards credit-based funding should accelerate this process in the direction of a celebration of this diversity, increasing opportunities for part-time students of all kinds.

Thirdly, the inter-relationship between the popular culture of our communities, economic regeneration, the concept of lifelong learning and university research is complex and constantly changing. The fact that 80 per cent of our current workforce will still be in place early in the next century and paradoxically 80 per cent of our technology will be outdated by the same period means we are facing a major socio-economic challenge. The population is ageing, the nature of employment is changing, communities are changing and the role of the State is changing. If we could focus on just two aspects of these inter-related issues: local and global perspectives. Research projects in the Department of Adult Continuing Education at Swansea, on community-based learning in former mining communities, on the future of the Welsh language amongst young adults, and women's training networks in Europe, all indicate the rapidity and challenge of change.

The collapse of male full-time employment has had paradoxical consequences with poor male adult education participation rates unless there is a recognition of locally-based learning opportunities which take account of received cultural patterns. Similarly, research into survival strategies for the Welsh language can best be developed by comparison with and linking to the experience of other so-called 'minoritised' cultures such as the Basque Country. Finally, research into alternative educational and training choices for women in former coalmining areas reveals that social and economic regeneration can be successfully achieved through small locally based and locally negotiated partnerships which are also simultaneously transnational. This wide-ranging research at Swansea should grow apace if we recognise the essential interface between university research and regional economic regeneration in a European context.

Finally, and perhaps most important of all, universities have a vital role to play in the development of a sense of active citizenship in a European and global context. One key factor in the creation of a democratic society is the extent to which people are socially included rather than socially excluded from knowledge, information, the dignity of work and lifelong educational opportunities. The European Union is increasingly concerned about the destabilisation of society through unemployment with the rise of drug abuse, racism and xenophobia as a result of such social exclusion: it is therefore imperative that university continuing education takes the lead in promoting the progressive social and employment policies of the European Union and in supporting equal opportunities initiatives in Wales such as Chwarae Teg, which acknowledge the diversity of people's needs.

The concept of a community university with an emphasis on strategic partnerships with employers, trade unions, local government, social movements, communities and above all adult learners is one way forward to address the growing democratic deficit in Wales. A strategic partnership with a democratised public broadcasting system, harnessing the new technologies of the information age to the historic and democratic ethos of Prifysgol y Werin could be a major educational contribution to the new millennium. The linking of undergraduate studies, graduate studies and research to the social and economic regeneration of the region could be another. In such ways the university will at last belong to the people, a citizens' university. The current revolution in British higher education, in the seismic shift towards a mass system, has created spaces for policy innovations such as the community university.

At a formal institutional level, a Mission Statement was signed on 23 April 1996 making a substantial commitment by Glamorgan, the Open University and Swansea to collaboration for the benefit of Valleys communities, at the very time that Government funding policies have tended towards accentuating secrecy and competition.

Beyond this, and equally significant, has been the creation of European-style social, local and regional partnerships. The Community University at Banwen has played a pivotal role in the development of the Dulais Valley Partnership embracing all local educational, business and voluntary bodies committed to community and economic regeneration, with advanced telecommunication links through BT sponsorship fulfilling a vital ingredient in the ongoing process. Similar initiatives are now developing in many parts of Britain, sometimes on the 'Banwen model' with, for example, Blaenau Ffestiniog in south Gwynedd reviving links during earlier industrial struggles in order to establish its own community-based learning opportunities.

II

Things International

8

Flying into History[*]

IN MAY 1979, JUST as Margaret Thatcher was forming her first Conservative Government pledged to roll back the State everywhere, I flew out to visit the US coalfields with six rank and file miners from the South Wales Valleys. What we saw was in many ways a glimpse of our own past and what we feared might be our future. It was also the collision of two cultures compounded by the sharing of what we thought to be a common language.

Within thirty-six hours of our arrival we had received two culture shocks: a meeting with Barbara Angle, author, single parent and woman miner – the first of many we were to encounter – with some discomfort. Secondly, and equally profound, was the small talk at a Mining Society dinner in Uniontown, Pennsylvania, which revealed a chasm in our understanding of 'our history':

> Coal-operator: I have been trying to clear my family name of any connection with the 'Molly Maguires'.
>
> Local mining student: Who were they? Were they those *radicals*?

---

[*] Whilst I wrote this article on 6 June 1988 for the now defunct *Cincinnati Post*, I have no evidence that it was ever published.

Re-reading a diary I kept from that trip, I noted that we had taken a decision from the outset 'to learn and to observe and not to judge'.

Much of what we witnessed and found difficult to accept out there has now either happened, is about to happen or has taken root. Most disturbingly, this was the distillation of the 'American Dream', of the cult of 'individualism', and was most recently in the 1980s identified here as the corrosive and amoral 'loads-of-money' ideology.

Yet, in 1979, in discussion with many of the men and women on the Appalachian coalfields, the same sense of decency, of a desire to help one another, of good neighbourliness, of struggling *collectively* for social justice existed in the coal communities there, as in our own country. Perhaps that collectivism, what we also call *solidarity*, was more comprehensive and rooted in our own coalfields because of the strength of mining unionism, of working-class political organisations and of communities themselves. Their inter-relationship, after all, had delivered public ownership of the mines and of many other industries in which closed union shops prevailed, as well as a socialist inspired Welfare State – all in those faraway days, full of hope, after the last war.

What we saw in the US were massively powerful energy corporations with worldwide and diverse economic interests, serious environmental problems caused by strip-mining, 'variable' safety and training standards, fragmented mining unionism, non-unionism and scab unionism, heavy coalfield unemployment in some districts and no sense of 'struggling for jobs *and* communities'.

We also witnessed the use of police and troops in industrial disputes in Harlan County and the emergence of women's employment in the mines which we initially wrongly perceived as a phenomenon encouraged and exploited by employers in an era of weak mining unionism.

After a decade of struggle, which has for the most part been led by the South Wales miners around a reassertion and re-definition of the 'right to work', 'the right to democratically run the industry in which we work', and 'the right to defend jobs so as to safeguard our communities', we are in the late 1980s in a broadly similar position to the US miners in the late 1970s.

What we are now witnessing is the possible eclipse of the two monoliths which have dominated the British coal industry for over forty years. The National Union of Mineworkers has lost more than half its membership since 1984 (down to less than 90,000 members) and is now confronted by a rival organisation, the so-called Union of 'Democratic' Mineworkers. The nationalised industry, run by British Coal, is faced with the prospect of privatisation within the next five years, sooner possibly, with the privatisation shortly of the electricity supply industry. These two measures will lead to further job losses and the destruction of more communities.

We are already being visited by US photographers and historians wishing to observe not only our diminishing number of mines and communities but our growing number of mining museums.

The era of coal being the major employer in so many of our coalfields in Britain and the US is admittedly now gone and is unlikely ever to return. We are now facing the prospect of thousands of former miners not earning a living ever again from coal – a prospect which has haunted US coalfields too, from West Virginia to Colorado. Yet people and communities remain and the desire for personal family and community improvement through collective action remains in both countries – despite recent bitter experiences.

As ever, a new generation of miners in South Wales and in the US, like their forebears – and their brothers and sisters in South Africa – are having to learn the hard way the lessons and virtues of union organisation, of unity, of discipline, and the need, above all, for a vision of the future. It may well be that the growth of energy corporations worldwide may also create its own gravediggers, as Zola's *Germinal* predicted, through a greater sense of universality among miners.

As Jim Bennet, a Pittsburgh miner, said to us on 16 May 1979:

> Regardless of language, miners are the same the world over. We have our political differences – that's good – it keeps you on your toes.

9

A Tribute to Will Lloyd, International Brigader (1914–1986)*

COMRADES AND FRIENDS,
We are here to express our personal sadness to the family of Will Lloyd but also to pay tribute to the life of a man who was widely respected locally and further afield for his service to the international working-class movement.

We bring to his surviving children, Linda, Gill, Ina and Byron and to Carol's family, to his nine grandchildren, his three great-grandchildren, his brother Harold and sister Margaret and all other relatives and friends, our deepest sympathies. Of all the organisations with which he was associated throughout his life, I have been asked in particular to convey the heartfelt sympathies of the International Brigades Association (Cymru) and the National Union of Mineworkers (South Wales Area).

Will Lloyd was born on 5 June 1914 in Aberaman into a world where poverty, unemployment and war and then revolution in Russia shaped a generation of activism in the South Wales Valleys which struggled for a better, decent life for their families, their communities and their class. Will Lloyd knew at first-hand

---

* Funeral Oration at Llwydcoed Crematorium, Aberdare, 2 December 1986.

the meaning of struggle. His father had died of malaria in 1923, contracted in Salonika during the Great War. His mother, known affectionately throughout the Aberdare valley, simply as 'Ma' Lloyd, reared her six children and was the profound political and moral influence on Will and helped make him, as she was, a tireless fighter against injustice.

At eight, he had joined the Communist Party's Young Pioneers. He once proudly told me that he had a Party card before even Arthur Horner. Edwin Greening once said, 'The Lloyds of Aberaman were in the Communist Party before the Paris Commune'. From 1923 onwards, he was active and remained active in the communist movement.

When he was twelve, he was distributing leaflets in the General Strike. At fourteen, he went to work at Shepherd's pit (Cwmaman) and then the Gadlys pit. At eighteen, he was victimised, along with the whole Federation lodge committee. It was the era of Powell Duffryn, known here and elsewhere as 'Poverty and Death'. Will Lloyd once said, with his usual directness, 'Powell Duffryn is Fascism'.

He now sought work in London. He became active in the anti-fascist movement and participated in the 'Battle of Cable Street' against the Blackshirts and also helped organise the welcome for the 1936 Hunger March.

General Franco's war against Spanish democracy had already begun and the young Will Lloyd, aged twenty-two, was among the very first British volunteers for the International Brigades. He fought alongside his friend, Bob Condon, the late Pat Murphy of Cardiff, the great Marxist writer Ralph Fox and the English poet John Cornford, in the desperate defence of Madrid. It was Christmastime 1936, before even a British battalion had been formed, and Will Lloyd was already in the front line against Fascism, three full years before the Second World War.

He later saw action as a runner in the battles of Jarama and Brunete. He returned home to a hero's welcome in the Aberdare valley in September 1937. But he, and all those International Brigaders who volunteered to fight for democracy in Spain, disliked such hero-worship. He was, if anything, a shy and retiring person. He had a dry, attractive sense of humour, always a ready smile, enjoyed good conversation and the company of his family and friends. He took great pride in his self-education, in the NCLC, the WEA, the Left Book Club and his period at Coleg Harlech.

After Spain, he continued to be active. He was a shop steward with the engineering union (AEU) at Rhigos during the last war and more recently was an official of the Penywaun Welfare Club. A friend and supporter of the Soviet Union all his life, he nevertheless was amongst the first to be critical of the cult of the personality.

Will Lloyd was a character, some would say a rough diamond. The last time I was in his company was just over a month ago, when he and other Welsh members of the International Brigades welcomed Paul Robeson Jr to Wales. Will and his family were so proud to meet the son of the late Paul Robeson who had sung at the memorial in Mountain Ash to the Welshmen who never returned from Spain. On that night in 1938 Robeson had said:

> I am here tonight because … I feel that in the struggle we are waging for a better life, an artist must do his part. I am here because I know that these fellows fought not only for Spain but for me and the whole world. I feel it is my duty to be here.

And so it is today for all of us – a duty and an honour to be here. We have come to pay tribute to Will Lloyd, an internationalist, like Paul Robeson, who fought for all of us.

His family will miss him – we shall all miss him.

We salute you, dear friend and comrade, for the last time, in the knowledge that you lived a full and purposeful life.

10

A Tribute to Eirie Pugh, sister of an International Brigader (1919–1993)*

G YFEILLION,
Rydym yn cwrdd yma heddiw i dalu teyrnged i'n chwaer Eirie Pugh, gynt o'r Onllwyn.

Friends,

We are here today to give thanks for and to pay tribute to the life of Eirie Pugh or Eirie Strangward as she is still affectionately known in her native Onllwyn.

First of all, can I extend our condolences to Eirie's family and friends who have been close to her all her life and have been so supportive in the last weeks. I have been asked by the family to pay particular tribute to the nursing staff of Tŷ Olwen whose care, as always, has been of the very best.

We are all shaped by the times in which we live and the communities into which we are born, grow up, learn and work. And in turn, we also in our different ways shape our times and our communities.

I am honoured to have been asked to speak at Eirie's funeral,

---

* Funeral Oration at Margam Crematorium, 1 July 1993.

particularly as it was her own wish. I am honoured because Eirie Pugh was one of those people where place and time and family come together. The two words 'Strangward' and 'Onllwyn' have a particular meaning for those of us who were born into the mining communities at the top end of the Dulais Valley in this century. Because for many they convey all that is best in Valley life: friendship, community, solidarity, concern for others, internationalism. Some of us would sum it up in the word 'Christian', others would call it 'socialist'. Whatever label we give to it, Eirie, in her own way, to those who knew her, her family and her friends, was all of this.

Our lives can often be seen as ever widening circles: I remember the Reverend Erastus Jones describing the closeness of the Dulais Valley in this way, of concentric circles, starting with the family.

Eirie was born in 1919 into a close-knit family, and a close-knit community of Back Row, Onllwyn. As the late Dan Lewis said, 'If a cat had kittens everyone would know, and no-one locked their doors.' But, they were difficult and dangerous times to bring up a large family and many was the time that Eirie remarked about the injustice of so many of her brothers who died young: Cyril, who died as a child; Ronald, killed at Onllwyn Colliery aged 17; and Jim, who died whilst fighting fascism in Spain with the International Brigades aged 26.

It was inevitable that many wanted to do something about such injustices as Jim had done, paying with his own life. That was why Eirie and her future husband, Urial, became socialists, indeed communists, because they were concerned about the injustices in our communities and universally. In her time, she was in the 1950s a very active local secretary of the British-Soviet Friendship Society.

There are two aspects of our lives, however, which are not public or political, in the way I have been describing, but essentially private. Women traditionally in Valley communities have had at least three roles: as carers, mothers and home makers – and that was indeed a central part of Eirie's life. When her mother died, she became a second mother for her brothers, and many years later she became a second mother for Clive; and later still, she nursed Urial during his last illness.

There was also her role as a wage earner, and she played her part along with many other women in the war effort at Rhigos and in the post-war period in a variety of situations.

And, perhaps that private aspect of her life – her lifelong friendships – is the one which reveals the person most. The warmth of that smile, and that radiant personality was recalled to me this week by her lifelong friends from Onllwyn in the 1920s through to Caewern in the 1990s.

Nancy Davies and Nancy Jones told me of her close circle of friends: on Monday ladies' nights, when they put the world to rights from the Government to the local buses, on Thursdays at Caewern Old Aged, lunch on Friday with the two Nancys and bingo in the Neath Empire.

That private part of her life – her family, her dressmaking classes, reciting in Onllwyn chapel and all her friendships – were crucial parts of her life, from beginning to end. Her friend Nancy Jones told me, 'remember to say she was a real lady: she was kind, cared about others, she was reserved, she was honest and she cared about our friendship'.

Eirie Pugh had the right values. She valued her family, her lifelong partnership with Urial; she valued her roots in Onllwyn and Caewern and she valued her friends and they her. And she also had clear universal values. She shared our dreams of a Jerusalem in the here and now, of social justice and of world peace. And through the life she led, she made her own contribution to realising that dream.

11

'Say Nothing and Leave in the Middle of the Night': The Spanish Civil War Revisited*

JUST OVER FIFTY YEARS ago in 1937 even isolated Gregynog in rural mid-Wales became caught up in the Spanish Civil War. A group of South Wales miners – mainly Communist – decided to lobby Stanley Baldwin, the Prime Minister – there on holiday – on the question of non-intervention and arms for the democratically elected Republican Government in Spain. One of those miners, Will Paynter, later to serve as a political commissar with the International Brigades, wrote of that incident at Gregynog nearly four decades later in his autobiography, *My Generation*:

> We knocked on the front door which was opened after a while by a maid who looked a mite apprehensive when she saw us. We said we would like to see Mr Baldwin and were told that he was out for the day. Had she been a man, I have no doubt that we would have staged a noisy scene of some kind, but such a demonstration was not on when confronted by a little Welsh maid. We hastily scribbled a note which we asked her to give

---

★ Published in *History Workshop Journal*, Vol. 2, Issue 1, 1991.

to Baldwin in which we stated our purpose and that we would call back the following day. We did go back next day but this time when we got to the opening in the trees we stopped not to admire the view, but because from behind the trees a number of men – plain-clothes policemen we later concluded – rushed at us, brandishing sticks. We were driven back and although we tried to take a picture of the charge, photography while resisting attack does not make for good results, and the picture was too blurred to reproduce. However, we got back to Newtown, held a meeting with the locals, and phoned the various newspapers and the BBC to give them the story, but the publicity our exploit received was disappointing.

That little incident was the prelude to an international struggle which has continued to engage the minds of historians and politicians alike. On the occasion of the Spanish Civil War's fiftieth anniversary, a large number of new and old books were published – many of which revise the way in which we use the evidence, often oral, of that pcriod.

This article is based on a paper given in 1986 to the Irish Labour History Society in Dublin, on the fiftieth anniversary of the outbreak of the Spanish Civil War. Questions from the floor ranged from suggestions of 'revisionism' to dealing with the minutiae of history rather than the 'great social and political movements of our time'.

It is sobering to begin on such a contemporary note because as historians, whether we like it or not, we evaluate the past through the eyes of the present. There is no purpose in denying such an organic link. In a Welsh play of the mid-1980s by Gareth Miles, entitled 'Unwaith Eto yng Nghymru Annwyl' ('Once Again in our Beloved Wales'), a much-imprisoned Welsh-language activist disappears for a whole year – without a word to his wife and children – seemingly to find a new way forward for Welsh nationalism following the defeat of the devolution referendum, by studying European civilisation in Paris and elsewhere.

That, however, was a cover. He had, in fact, joined the armed struggle against apartheid in South Africa. He returns without warning, pursued by BOSS, the South African state secret police. In a blaze of publicity, he explains to Wales and the world through the Welsh media, why he had joined the ANC. At the very end of the play he talks to his wife about their lives:

> 'Have you missed me? Have the children missed me?' 'No, not really,' she says. She explains that during his absence she has discovered herself and her own feminist politics. She announces that she is leaving him to join a group of like-minded women.

That play, of course, was greatly influenced by the women's movement of the 1980s (particularly Greenham) and there is no doubt in my mind that, in reflecting again on the 1930s, the emotions which we denied consciously or unconsciously in the 1970s, need to be recognised and written about. This is not to say that the women's role in the miners' strike of 1984–85 was either revelatory or in any way historically significant. It is still too early to quantify such changes: a more considered assessment is, however, now possible although conclusions may well be deemed to be 'revisionist' in the worst sense of the word.

I write here of my work on the South Wales miners and the Spanish Civil War. The research I did on this subject was mostly undertaken in the late 1960s and throughout most of the 1970s, although my book, *Miners Against Fascism*, was not published until 1984. I am not sure now whether it suffered or benefited from this gestation.

In the two decades which have passed since I started this work, Franco and Francoism have thankfully gone. So have most of the Welsh International Brigaders whom I had the privilege of meeting and knowing: some, I am proud to say, became quite close friends.

What I have to say is by way of a reassessment – not revisionism I trust – of at least some of that research.

It is natural in times of great human crisis, in times of war, indeed *any* war, to emphasise the courage and the principled heroism of those men who were prepared to die for a cause. That is how it was, and has been, in the way we see the men from all over the world who went to defend democracy in Spain between 1936 and 1938 by joining the International Brigades. So many of those nationalities have yet to be acknowledged. For example, the Jewish contribution (18 per cent overall), calculated to be the largest single response. The Welsh response is typified in a poem by the Welsh revolutionary dentist T. E. Nicholas, entitled 'In Memory of a Welshman Who Fell in Spain' which concludes:

> … and now amid
> Those nameless ones who shared that dream
> He lies, who died for Wales outside Madrid.

That is all true. 'Dole' and 'jail' did characterise the bulk of the Welsh volunteers. They had experienced years of unemployment, victimisation, long and bitter strikes, hunger marches and indeed prison sentences for their trade union, community and political activities. They saw 'Spain' as but an extension of their struggles in the Valleys. As one volunteer, Lance Rogers, recalled:

> It was a continuing process. Here we were in Merthyr Tydfil in a continuing struggle night and day. The Hunger March over, we left for the Spanish War. It was a fulfilment and a most natural step to take.

But that is only part of the story. I believe we do a great disservice to the volunteers and to history if we merely dwell on this timeless manly, macho 'going off to war' which has always been with us from the Crusades to the Falklands and the Gulf.

Glorification of war, all wars, including 'just' wars, invariably, inevitably and sometimes deliberately omits the personal and family traumas, emotions and sacrifices. We know of *men's* responses, at least the so-called *manly* or *macho* responses but what of the women – the wives, mothers and sisters? What of their anxieties, bitterness, heroism? And what of the men's so-called less *manly* or *macho* responses? We often refer to the International Brigades as being lost to history, until recent times. What of the women who made it possible for them to go? Have they not been lost? This is not to allege personal neglect by the combatants but to suggest that we, as historians, have not asked the right questions about Spain and the 1930s. For example, I was always reluctant to visit widows or close female relatives of volunteers who had been killed in action, often, I should say in my own defence, being warned against such visits by well-meaning party comrades.

One famous survivor of the war, Cardiff seaman Pat Murphy (born in Cumberland of Newry and Dundalk parents), once cautioned me in a letter in 1970:

> … it's a bit touchy visiting these relatives as one often gets some nasty remarks instead of compliments. I've had some during my activities as relatives are not always enthusiastic about us.

But not to face the unacceptable, the unpleasant and the unpalatable and only to deal with the convenient is to distort history. It is like writing a history of the 1984–85 miners' strike by only talking to the pickets, ignoring those on strike who were never active, those who broke with the strike, to say nothing of the wives of all of them, the managers, the colliery officials and the police. There was a heroic story to be told but there was also a darker side, which unfortunately does not always conveniently fit into our scheme of things.

Within the whole tortuous process of volunteering for Spain is to be found a far more important human problem than even the requirement of obvious heroism on the battlefields themselves. Take the decision of Irene and Will Paynter, two dedicated Rhondda Communists, newly married, faced with the problem of the party asking him to volunteer because it was politically necessary to have a leading Communist to assist in the changeover in battalion leadership. He returned to Britain once this had been achieved in late 1937. Their private, personal drama was experienced by many who went to Spain. Theirs was to become all the more poignant. Irene died in childbirth in 1939. Will Paynter disliked hero-worship and talking of his experiences: 'I was never a soldier,' he would often say. He even disliked International Brigade reunions. He was more concerned with the future than the past. The past was so full of pain – his own and that of others – particularly as he had to deal with the human problems of desertion and demoralisation at the front.

He reported directly to Harry Pollitt, general secretary of the Communist Party of Great Britain at the time. In one letter, on 30 May 1937, he wrote:

> Repatriation is still the big question for us … I am getting as hard faced as an undertaker … anxiety is caused by letters from home. Plaintive letters pleading with husbands and sons to come home. This I feel is a reflection upon the work of the local people at home … Relatives are not made to feel proud that their menfolk are out here. If they were, the letters would be encouraging and inspiring and have the reverse affect.
>
> Therefore the question of leave is not merely a question of 'humanity' it is a military and political question and the factors that govern that at the moment are known to you.

Later, on 9 June 1937, he wrote of the underlying problems of desertion. He acknowledged that 'there were some good types here' amongst the deserters. He believed the real problems were long periods in the line, 'very bad types' sent out early on; weaknesses of political work in the battalion; and wrong information in Britain 'based upon the conception that all that is necessary is to get them out, then let things take their course'. He complained particularly of inconsistency in the giving of leave back to Britain and of the *Daily Worker* actually reporting meetings back home where 'deserters' were speaking.

For all his worries he ended his letter:

> Apart from dissentry [*sic*], gutsache, headaches, stiff joints, skin itches and weariness, everyone is in the pink.

Such glimpses of life inside and outside the battalion rarely appear in official military histories. But do they not reveal genuine and understandable human anxieties and stresses under conditions of war? The official history of the British battalion makes no use at all of Paynter's letters. What also of the letters from families and friends? Unfortunately, most of these letters would have been lost through the normal ravages of war. One collection of letters from home returned to Wales via the USA with Paul Robeson, when he presented them to the family of Jim Strangward, killed in the battle of the Ebro. Others naturally suffered at the hands of the International Brigade censor. How then do we reconstruct a picture of the effect of volunteering and military service on the 'women folk', as they were called, and their families?

For many families – often 'Communist families' – volunteering was seen as natural and 'accepted'. 'Ma' Lloyd and 'Crid' Brown were leaders of the Communist Party in the Aberdare Valley. For their sons *not* to go, whilst encouraging others, would have been odd. And so it was with many other, similar families. Jim Brewer, a Labour Party member, wrote to tell his parents that it was inevitable for him to go, given he was the third generation of socialists in a family whose antecedents included Chartists. But that is not to say that there were no tensions, no personal anxieties. Frank Owen, killed at Brunete, wrote to his wife of the decision they had taken together. But clearly in response to her letters, he ended what was to be his last with some reassurances:

> You ask when I am coming home, I cannot say as no-one knows, but please do not worry, as I have told you before, there is no need for it, be a little patient, as you say 'All will end well' … Well, Charlotte, I have not much more to write about, but before I close I wish to impress upon you not to worry. Tell my mother and the rest of the family likewise, because I am OK. In conclusion I wish to you all the best. Bye for the present and Cheerio to the kids, and the rest.
>   Your husband Frank.

Perhaps the most authentic and enduring voice on the subject, ironically we might say, comes from the fiction of the time. Lewis Jones, Communist councillor and leader of the unemployed, knew better than anyone the meaning of 'Spain'. He had volunteered early in the war but had been turned down because he was too valuable as a propagandist back home; so many of his friends had volunteered and some had been killed; he was surrounded by their wives, their widows and their families; and in the last desperate months he could barely cope with the personal anguish of the Communist Party recruiting young men for what appeared inevitable death:

> 'You have no right to ask for such sacrifices,' he told Billy Griffiths, recruiting in the Rhondda in the spring of 1938. Lewis Jones died the week Barcelona fell to Franco and on the day he died he addressed over thirty Spanish Aid street meetings.

He wrote of his feelings in his posthumously published novel,

We Live. It is very likely that the last two chapters were completed by his close friend Mavis Llewellyn, who would have given the book such an unusually frank and, some would say, feminist ending.

In a scene clearly drawn from his own experiences he describes the feelings of Mary, the wife of a future volunteer (a character clearly based on Mavis Llewellyn) in the penultimate chapter of *We Live,* suitably entitled, 'A Party Decision'. When she was told, in a closed Communist Party meeting that no military training was necessary for volunteers (her husband had none), she gasped:

> 'Ah.' The sound escaped from Mary's lips like the sign of a mother who suddenly feels again the long dissolved grief of the parting from her child.

If volunteering was difficult to reconcile for the politically active women, what of those who were apolitical? In such a situation, the instruction to volunteers was simple, brutal but necessary: 'say nothing and leave in the middle of the night.' One volunteer was about to be married, the word got out and the family prevented his departure. But for so many wives and mothers we shall never fully know the depths of their despair. Harry Stratton left a pregnant wife without telling her. He never heard from her the whole time he was in Spain, such was her anger and despair. He was not to know until his return that the baby had miscarried. Tim Harrington was another who left without a word. Unemployed for over eight years, he and others from the valleys of South Wales felt that they were economic burdens to their families. They believed they were of more use to Spain than to their families. On his return over a year later, his wife and three children were surviving by picking fruit. Nan Green, a returned nurse from Spain, then working for the International Brigades Dependents' Aid Fund, recalled thirty years later the poignant homecoming. When her husband arrived, having walked through fields to his wife and children, she shunned him. It was as if she had reconciled herself to his death.

And so it was with so many other volunteers, painful departures and, if lucky, still painful homecomings. Sid James left his mother on her deathbed. She died not knowing that he had already been killed. Tom Jones' parents both died before his three-year ordeal in a Franco prison under sentence of death had ended. He returned to find his insurance death benefit his parents had claimed, in a drawer, never having been spent.

And Billy Griffiths departed, leaving his widowed mother caring for his only daughter who was still at school. His torment must have been the torment of thousands, but rarely has it been captured or, for that matter, publicly admitted. His mother could not understand:

> She was heartbroken. To hide my feelings, I tore myself away from the house with the curtest of goodbyes … Looking back it seemed cruel and heartless but at the time it was something I had to do … Yet I hesitated to take the final step. Was it fear? Up to a point, yes. I hated violence. Yet I was no pacifist. Somehow I did not quite fit into an army. I had neither the physique nor the temperament to make a good soldier. In my opinion there were others far better fitted for this role than I … I resented being asked to go to Spain. Why me? Could I be spared? Alas for my conceit everyone agreed that I should go. I was not indispensable. It was only then that I began to look at the problem with open eyes. Politics was no longer a game. Slogans became clothed in flesh and blood. What one believed in one must be prepared to die for. It was a sobering thought …

This brings me back to my original assessment, which after a lifetime of studying such men – and now belatedly such women – I am proud to say is generally unchanged. The acceptance and realisation that they all had their human frailties and doubts merely underlines the enormity of their sacrifices. A romantic view of the war is not necessary.

That is why they are still revered in the South Wales Valleys and that is why on 12 July 1986, in Ystrad Rhondda, they were the guests of honour at a benefit dinner for Nicaraguan Solidarity along with the Nicaraguan Ambassador and veterans of the Spanish Republican Army.

Yet serious questions remain. How did all this personal turmoil affect gender relations? Did the unhappiness, the bitterness, as well as the undoubted pride, raise questions about such sacrifices? There is no doubt that there was a difference between those families who welcomed their sons home and those who did not. The popular memory in the Valleys rightly characterises International Brigaders as heroes, but is it also selective? Does our collective 'class' memory remove such 'minutiae'? If so, why? These are difficult questions but they need asking, otherwise we reduce our history to a series of glorious episodes which have little to do with the past.

The next time we study a 'just war' it might be wiser to start from the premise that there is nothing *manly* about such human dramas. Indeed, it might be instructive for a socialist feminist to write it.

12

A Celebration of the Life of Espe: Esperanza Careaga James (1931– 2004)

'A life of hope, in the Basque Country and Wales'*

W<small>E ARE ALL HERE</small> today as family and friends of Espe, to give thanks for her life and her love.

We are here to embrace Alan, Ceri and Karl and their families and the family too in Spain, particularly her brother Alberto and her sister Trudi and brother-in-law Brian in Australia.

Espe's life was one of tragedy and happiness both in Spain and Wales. Her name, Esperanza – Hope – expresses so well the courage and love of Espe's life and that of her two families.

I had two things in common with Espe.

We were both children of miners who were communists and whose lives were changed totally and forever by the Spanish Civil War. And we both were fortunate to become part of the Harris family of Barry – free thinkers, theatre performers, socialists, communists, youth hostellers, cyclists, anti-fascists. Mair, my

---

* Funeral Oration at Roath Court, Cardiff, December 2004.

wife, was Espe's first cousin and Espe's nursery nurse at Gladstone Road School.

What I have to say today is based in large part on Alan's notes and his and Espe's research into her family life.

Ignacio Careaga Baztarrica and Guillerma Galíndez Gómez were a happily married Basque couple living in a small village, Gallarta, just north-west of Bilbao and overlooking the harbour of Santurtzi where today the P&O ferry from the UK berths.

This was a mining area and Espe's father was most likely employed as a miner extracting iron ore. In November 1929 their first child, a boy named Alberto, was born and then in May 1931, Espe. A second boy, Amador, was born in 1936. The happy, normal day-to-day life of the family was destroyed by the onset of the Spanish Civil War in 1936.

Espe's father joined the Basque army to fight the Fascist army of Franco. He was a Communist and a political commissar in this army.

History records the many tragic events of this war.

In July 1936, the Spanish Prime Minister requested aid to fight the uprising by Franco. France agreed but then in August the UK government signed a non-intervention pact with France, Russia, Germany and Italy.

It was obvious that Nazi Germany and Fascist Italy wanted the fascists to win the war, and in the UK many in the Labour Party and other anti-fascists began the call for military support for the democratically elected Spanish Popular Front Government. We have all heard of the International Brigades with many South Wales miners going to Spain to help the fight against Fascism.

In April 1937 Franco's forces began their northern offensive and the German and Italian air forces began bombing the Basque towns culminating in the saturation bombing by the Luftwaffe of the non-militarised Basque town of Guernica on 26 April 1937, made famous later by Picasso's mural.

Requests for the children to be evacuated were denied by the British Government, but the Archbishop of Canterbury had been in the Basque region and his testimony of the harrowing plight of the children so stirred up the ire of the British public that the Government had to agree to allow the children into the UK. But the Government refused to have anything to do with their welfare.

Manuel Moreno, whose mother was one of the children, later wrote recalling the generosity of the British people: 'This was the first time in British history that the British people opened their arms and hearts en masse to say, "We will care for you".'

In Spain the children were taken to the Bilbao quayside in trainloads of six hundred, amid emotional scenes of family distress. Throughout Thursday, 20 May, the SS *Habana* was loaded with its young cargo. Espe was with her brother Alberto and officialdom separated them: Espe onto the boat and Alberto onto a train and on to Russia. Espe was eight days before her sixth birthday and alone amongst four thousand children. It was to be fifty years before she would meet her brother again.

After the SS *Habana* sailed − her master Captain Ricardo Fernandez had already made two trips with refugees to France and he and the crew were exhausted − they were met by HMS *Royal Oak* and HMS *Forester*, who escorted the *Habana* to Southampton: in those days a 48-hour rough voyage.

On sighting England, the children were shouting, 'Viva Inglaterra' and had recovered their good spirits to become excited at the thought of safety in a new strange land.

On the Saturday evening, 22 May, the *Habana* anchored off Fawley, and on Sunday the children were medically examined and labelled before being brought ashore and given hot baths and a change of clothing. It was pouring with rain when the first children arrived at the tented camp at Stoneham set up in a field donated by local farmer G. H. Brown. This camp had been set up in just three weeks by the local residents and Southampton was alive with offers of help.

The word went out that the children were in need of food and clothes supplies. Schoolchildren made it their task to collect and donate eggs. One thousand people met at Southampton Guildhall and pledged their help and money. The local branch of the Co-op donated food and clothes.

Four thousand children were introduced to their new home, row upon row of tents, and the positioning of the tents being decided by the political persuasions of the families. The children aged between four and fifteen years were settled in and played happily. One problem arose, and the local paper at the time reports that the local flying club had been requested not to fly near the camp as the planes were terrifying the children.

The local residents thought the camp was for a short period but it remained for two years.

Nearly every part of the UK accepted their quota of children: there were 94 Basque colonies, and wherever these were sited the local people rose to the occasion and supported the children.

The colony of longest duration in Wales was at Cambria House in Caerleon, and Mrs Fernandez of Dowlais became warden. The children formed a football team and a dancing troupe for Spanish Aid. The Harris family believed that the photograph on the milk tokens to raise funds was that of Espe.

In my book *Miners Against Fascism* I wrote:

> The teachers [at Caerleon] found that several of the children were talented musicians and dancers so that concerts throughout South Wales were organised in which Spanish and Basque folk songs and dances were the main attraction.

Espe was one such child who entered the warm embrace of South Wales. It was said that her particular Basque roots could be located by the dances she performed.

By 1939 the war was over and the repatriation started, but only of those children who had a family to go back to. Four hundred children never returned. Espe was one of those. Her father Ignacio and his comrades had been captured by Italians as they were about to escape from the port of Santander. He and many others were imprisoned at Pamplona in appalling conditions and later he and many other prisoners mysteriously disappeared. Her mother was with the baby Amador and was in poor health and almost destitute. She later remarried. Alberto returned home and, in due course, Espe had two step-brothers she never saw.

Guillerma died on 26 October 1962, aged just 59. She never saw Espe again, but she knew she was being well cared for and settled into life in Barry and Cardiff.

George and Gert Harris were active in Barry collecting money for the Basque children and when the occasion arose they accepted Espe as a member of their family in 282 Barry Road, where Espe arrived on 23 December 1939. The UK was now at war with Germany and considering the times and what lay ahead, George and Gert's fostering of Espe was quite a remarkable and generous gesture.

13

Paul Robeson:
His Legacy for Wales*

Pan ddechreuais i ar y daith hir o baratoi'r ddarlith hon i esbonio etifeddiaeth Paul Robeson yng Nghymru, roeddwn yn ymwybodol o'r effaith a gafodd ar fywydau miloedd ar filoedd o bobl yng Nghymru. Ac wrth gwrs roedd cadarnhad o hyn yn llwyddiant arbennig yr arddangosfa 'Gadewch i Paul Robeson Ganu!' Dim ond dieithryn yng Nghymru all ddweud heddiw, 'Pwy yw Paul Robeson?'

Ga i dalu teyrnged nawr ar y cychwyn i Beverley Humphreys a Phil Cope, cyfeillion ac artistaid hynod, am eu gwasanaeth yn y frwydr dros yr arddangosfa?

Ond dim ond wrth orffen paratoi'r ddarlith y sylweddolais pa mor bwysig oedd Paul Robeson yn fy mywyd i, ac ym mywyd fy nhad, ac hefyd i ba raddau yr oedd ein gweledigaeth wedi cael ei heffeithio gan ei fywyd a'i egwyddorion, yn enwedig ei gysylltiad â Chymru.

When I began to prepare this lecture on the legacy of Paul Robeson in Wales, I knew from personal experience how much

---

* A lecture given to the Friends of the National Library of Wales, Aberystwyth, on 12 July 2003, first published in English in *The Bevan Foundation Review*, Issue 3, Winter 2003/04, and in Welsh in Daniel G. Williams (gol./ed.), *Canu Caeth: Y Cymry a'r Affro-Americaniaid* (Gomer, 2010).

he touched the lives of so many people. This knowledge was re-affirmed many times over with the outstanding success of the exhibition 'Let Paul Robeson Sing!' and could I at the outset pay tribute to Phil Cope and Beverley Humphreys, friends and remarkable artists, in their efforts and sacrifices in making this exhibition possible?

What I did not know until the moment I completed the preparation of this lecture was how profound an impact he had on my own life and that of my father and how our view of Wales and the world was influenced by his life and his relationship to us and to our country.

I suppose when my father and I stood in silence at the all-night vigil at Llandaff Cathedral in 1964 organised by Bishop Glyn Simon in support of the ANC leaders Nelson Mandela and Walter Sisulu who were potentially under sentence of death, our awareness of their cause had been highlighted by the words and actions of Paul Robeson decades before.

For this and many other reasons only a stranger to Wales today would dare say 'Who is Paul Robeson?'

Memories and movements

Banners are the 'memory of a movement': that's what the late Professor Gwyn Alf Williams was fond of telling us.

When Nelson Mandela visited London following his release from prison he was welcomed to the Shadow Cabinet room by Neil Kinnock. Pride of place then in that room was given to the banner of the Abercraf miners with its slogan, 'Mewn Undeb mae Nerth a Heddwch' (In Unity there is Strength and Peace). And so also there is pride of place for the banner in the exhibition 'Let Paul Robeson Sing!'

'Why are the black and white miners together?' was the distinguished visitor's question.

'That's simple,' was Neil Kinnock's reply. 'This is a South Wales miners' banner!'

'Yes, of course, I understand,' was Nelson Mandela's reply. He understood because the South Wales miners had been so prominent in the long campaign for his release.

The banner was redolent with history. Indeed, it was the 'memory' of many converging movements. It was made in the year after the Sharpeville Massacre, in the red, green and gold colours of the African National Congress and within the cosmopolitan community of Abercraf which had welcomed Spanish and Portuguese miners into its midst before 1914, and after 1936 had sent several of its sons to fight fascism in Spain with the International Brigades.

Heavy in symbolism, it encapsulated many interlinked movements – the miners, peace, internationalism, and at that very moment, the newly emerging anti-apartheid movements in South Africa, Wales and throughout the world.

It was at that moment too, in 1960, that I heard Paul Robeson sing live for the last time in the Royal Festival Hall, significantly with a Welsh male voice choir, Côr Meibion Cwmbach, and significantly too at a concert of another vital progressive movement, the Movement for Colonial Freedom.

This international link between the South Wales miners and Paul Robeson, and then in turn with Nelson Mandela, is of some considerable historical significance. Indeed, I would contend that the unique relationship between Paul Robeson and the mining communities of South Wales, and Wales more widely, forged between the 1920s and the 1950s, was a major contributing factor in developing in Wales from the 1960s to the 1990s one of the strongest and broadest anti-apartheid movements in the world. When Nelson Mandela received the freedom of the city of Cardiff in 1998 he acknowledged the vital role played by the South Wales miners in gaining his release and in the anti-apartheid struggle more generally.

The purpose of this lecture then is to explore that Paul

Robeson legacy for Wales, which manifested itself most profoundly in recent decades through the Welsh Anti-Apartheid Movement, a legacy which owed much to his awareness raising of the earlier anti-colonial struggles.

Shared values

Paul Robeson was born the son of a runaway slave in 1898, the same year as the founding of the South Wales Miners' Federation.

There are striking similarities between the life and ideals of Paul Robeson and those of the miners' union in South Wales. It is therefore not surprising that the man and the organisation became intertwined, indeed inseparable for nearly five decades. My father, the late Dai Francis, wrote of Paul Robeson's links with the South Wales miners at the time of his death in January 1976, shortly before they were due to renew their friendship in the United States.

My father's tribute, entitled 'Paul Robeson: Cyfaill Cymru a'r Byd' (Paul Robeson: Friend of Wales and the World) was published in the Welsh-language magazine *Y Saeth* in the summer of 1976. What was it that drew the man to a working-class community, divided as they were by a great ocean and seemingly very different cultures?

He always acknowledged that it was in Wales that he 'first understood the struggle of white and Negro together'. In the crucial decades of his life from the 1920s to the 1950s he shared the same world vision as the miners' union in South Wales. They were both rooted in their people and in their communities and they always acknowledged their history. They both believed in the universal struggle for social justice and world peace. They both celebrated the cultures of humankind by emphasizing the inseparability of politics, culture and life that came together so dramatically in the 1930s and the 1950s.

They both recognized the right of every citizen throughout the world to have what Paul Robeson called in 1957 'dignified and abundant lives'.

And perhaps most important of all, they both attached great value in recognizing that our struggles at home and abroad were indivisible.

When Paul Robeson spoke to Australian workers in 1960 he referred to the Welsh miners he had met on hunger marches in the 1930s. He said he had learnt so much from their spirited, principled struggles for justice and their fine sense of solidarity. 'You are on our side, Paul,' he recalled them saying.

That sense of identity and identification is very important from the moment he met unemployed Welsh miners singing in Trafalgar Square in 1929 and then visited them in the Rhondda and the Talygarn Miners' Rest Home. Throughout the 1930s their cause became his cause. In the early 1930s he also sang at Caernarfon, Wrexham, Neath, and many other smaller towns. And then there were the two defining moments at Mountain Ash in 1938 and the Rhondda in 1939.

At the Mountain Ash Memorial Concert to the Welshmen who died fighting fascism in Spain, he said:

I have waited a long time to come down to Wales – because I know there are friends here … I am here tonight because as I have said many times before, I feel that in the struggle we are waging for a better life an artist must do his part.

And then in 1939 he starred in *The Proud Valley*, which depicted graphically the struggles of the South Wales miners. It was the film that approximated best to his own values and his own views.

These two 'public statements' in the Valleys of South Wales defined the man and his ideals. He identified himself with our cause. One of the great artists of the world was saying that the besieged mining communities of South Wales were not alone.

Nearly twenty years later, my father's speech at a 'Let Paul Robeson sing!' conference in London's St Pancras Town Hall referred to the Mountain Ash gathering in 1938 and was reported in this way:

> ... his [my father's] was one of the first organisations to raise the issue of Robeson's denial of a passport. He recalled Robeson surrounded by children welcoming the returning International Brigades home from Spain. He could never forget that, but he had no children then, and now he wanted his son to have the chance to see and hear Robeson.

I read that document alongside letters of solidarity and support from President Nkrumah of Ghana, Charlie Chaplin and the Chilean poet Pablo Neruda in the Robeson archives at Howard University in Washington.

And wider struggles beyond Europe

In associating himself with the mining communities of South Wales, Paul Robeson also inevitably raised in those communities awareness of injustice elsewhere in the world, from America's Deep South to the persecution of Jews in Nazi Germany, and the plight of colonial peoples in Africa and Asia, even before there were anti-colonial movements.

It is acknowledged that when he lived in London in the 1930s he became acquainted with and learnt much from black African and Afro-Caribbean thinkers and political activists. He, of course, met Jomo Kenyatta, but there were many others who in turn often spoke and campaigned in the South Wales Valleys in this period.

The West Indian Marxists C. L. R. James and George Padmore visited Briton Ferry and the Dulais Valley in the late 1930s. Indeed, James reputedly completed his masterpiece *Black Jacobins* in the home of the Creunant headteacher Brinley Griffiths, whilst future Indian Foreign Minister Krishna Menon spoke at Onllwyn in the 1940s for the India League and British Guyana's first Prime Minister Cheddi Jagan spoke at Ystradgynlais in the early 1950s. The Russian-American anarchist Emma Goldman married James Colton, the Amman Valley miner whose correspondence is preserved in the National Library of Wales. She was a frequent speaker in South Wales in the inter-war period on many radical and revolutionary topics, including anti-colonialism.

Paul Robeson was part of the group of talented black political thinkers and activists who from the late 1930s broadened the political horizons of Welsh miners beyond those mythical 'barricades from Tonypandy to Madrid'. The South Wales miners became aware of these anti-colonial perspectives which developed into movements in the early 1940s and 1950s and reached a crisis point in the 1960s with the beginnings of the armed struggle against apartheid.

Paul Robeson re-entered the global stage after the Second World War to speak out against colonialism abroad and the lack of civil rights at home. And that is why he was feared by some and admired by many on so many continents.

Recently released Home Office files show that his linking of domestic and international politics and his specific championing of anti-colonialism meant that the secret services in Britain and the US became alarmed by his unique ability to help build a bridge between the emerging American civil rights movement and the black anti-colonial politicians of the West Indies and Africa, with whom he had been associated for over a decade. More than that, he was raising a wider awareness by linking these struggles with the trade union and labour movement, over a decade before Martin Luther King made that important link, ultimately a fatal one for him.

In May 1945 Paul Robeson appealed for $40,000 as chairman of the American Council for African Affairs. The Home Office files reveal that the head of MI5 was complaining that Paul Robeson's organization had communist links and was making 'ill-informed' complaints about Britain's colonial administration.

In 1949 and 1950 he was 'tracked' by MI5 when he visited Britain and in 1951, by which time his passport had been withdrawn, an MI5 report stated:

Robeson when last over here was a security nuisance. He is convinced he has a mission to heed oppressed Negroes and colonial peoples everywhere. He is a fanatical communist and intensely ambitious ... we think you will agree this is a case where it would be advisable on security grounds to refuse leave to land should he attempt to enter the UK.

There is no doubt that his uncompromising views shook both the US and the British Governments. This is illustrated in a speech he prepared for broadcast on 23 September 1946. He said:

I stand here ashamed. Ashamed that it is necessary eighty-four years after Abraham Lincoln signed the Emancipation Proclamation, it is necessary to rebuild the democratic spirit that brought that document into being ... I speak of the wave of lynch terror, and mob assault against Negro Americans. Since V. J. Day, scores have been victims, most of whom were veterans, and even women and children.

But I am not ashamed to stand here as a servant of my people, as a citizen of America, to defend and fight for the dignity and democratic rights of Negro Americans ... to fight for their right to live.

For such speeches in the coming four years, he was banned

from theatres and radio broadcasts and ultimately from travelling abroad for most of the 1950s.

The campaign for the return of his passport, which lasted for almost a decade and extended across the world, involving old friends and now world statesmen like Nehru of India and Nkrumah of Ghana, had as one of its main centres the South Wales coalfield. This was only to be expected.

The transatlantic link between New York and the South Wales Miners' Eisteddfod in 1957 has become part of Welsh popular memory. I was there when Paul Robeson sang to us and I was there again when Paul Robeson finally arrived in 1958, having already visited the National Eisteddfod in Ebbw Vale as the guest of the local MP Aneurin Bevan.

His welcome to the Eisteddfodau indicated the breadth of his popular support in Wales. Whilst his links were specific to the Valleys of the south over a period of nearly three decades, his appeal as an artist, civil rights campaigner and humanitarian extended across the whole of Wales. This was summed up by his request for a Welsh hymn book at Ebbw Vale because its music reminded him so much of his own people.

He had, of course, his strong personal contacts and friendships with the black community in Cardiff's Butetown, as indicated by the telegram to wish him well before his first night at Stratford in 1958: 'Cardiff Coloured send best wishes for success, A. Shepherd 213 Bute Street.'

And, long before he returned to Wales, a fan letter from Aberystwyth which read:

> I am eager to arrange a concert here where you have so many admirers … I can assure you that your visit to Aberystwyth would be looked forward to more eagerly that I could ever let you know.
>   Yours most sincerely and in great admiration,
>   Horace G. Thomas, Terminus Hotel, Terrace Road,
>   Aberystwyth.

1981: A defining moment for Wales and apartheid

The spring of 1981 was a poignant and painful time for me on a personal level. My father died on 30 March and shortly afterwards Côr Meibion Cwmbach decided to visit apartheid South Africa. My father was president of the choir and of the Wales Anti-Apartheid Movement; I participated in the ultimately successful campaign to prevent the visit, and in that campaign Paul Robeson's enduring memory was evoked many times, along with a powerful message from his son, Paul Robeson Jr. The campaign, embracing political parties, unions, churches and indeed choristers, was summed up by the human rights activist, the Bishop of Namibia-in-exile, Dr Colin Winter, whose powerful letter to the choir was distributed throughout the campaign.

At a meeting which I addressed in Aberdare on 21 July 1981, attended by Hanif Bhamjee, who came to personify the anti-apartheid struggle in Wales for nearly two decades, I quoted from Paul Robeson's 1953 speech at the Peace Arch on the US-Canadian border. The speech brought together all the universal values and struggles which he and progressive opinion in Wales and South Africa had come to represent. He said:

> We who labour in the arts … must remember that we come from the people, our strength comes from the people and we must serve the people and be part of them.
>
> I received an invitation that could not mean more [to the Miners' Eisteddfod] from the miners in Wales … where I first understood the struggles of white and Negro together … They feel me a part of that land. For many years I have been struggling for the independence of the colonial peoples of Africa … I am proud of the America in which I was born. My father was a slave reared in North Carolina. I have many friends all over the earth and rightly so …
>
> My people are determined in America … to be first-class citizens … and that is the rock upon which I stand. From that rock I reach out … across the world to my forefathers in Africa

… because I know that there is one humanity and that all human beings can live in full human dignity and in friendship.

Paul Robeson was one of the few human rights campaigners of his era, long before the civil rights movement, to have such a world view, capable of highlighting injustice wherever it existed, including South Africa, long before apartheid had been institutionalized by the South African state. His challenging words on South Africa in 1950 helped prepare the early ground for the anti-apartheid movement across the world, including Wales:

> … for all their pass laws, for all their native compounds, for all their Hitler-inspired registration of natives and non-whites, the little clique that rules South Africa is baying at the moon. For it is later than they think in the procession of history, and that rich land must one day soon return to the natives on whose backs the proud skyscrapers of the Johannesburg rich were built.

An enduring legacy

As Paul Robeson's political activism and artistic career were drawing to a close in the early 1960s the struggle against apartheid was only beginning. Nelson Mandela, Walter Sisulu and their comrades were also beginning their long prison sentences. Paul Robeson's contribution to Wales and the world can be measured in many ways and not least in the way he broadened our horizons to prepare for the anti-racist and anti-colonial struggles which were to focus so sharply on southern Africa. The breadth of the Wales Anti-Apartheid Movement embracing trade unions, churches and all shades of progressive opinion owed much to the universal ideas of peace, dignity and abundance about which he spoke so eloquently to us through that transatlantic link from New York to Porthcawl in 1957.

I am reminded of the eloquent words of T. J. Davies in his moving tribute to Paul Robeson, published in 1981:

Pan ddisgynnodd y pridd arno, a'r lludw i'r lludw, symbol oedd o'r lluchio baw a phridd. Ni chafodd neb fwy, eto ni lwyddodd lluchio baw llywodraeth ei dawelu, ac ni thawelwyd mohono gan y pridd olaf. Mae'n dal i ganu. Mae'n dal i ysbrydoli. Mae'n fwy byw heddiw nag erioed. Trechodd.

[When Paul Robeson finally died no Government had succeeded in silencing him. He continues to sing. He continues to inspire. He is more alive today than ever. He overcame all in the end.]

Fel dywedodd fy nhad, 'Cyfaill Cymru a'r Byd'.

My father described Paul Robeson on his death as, 'A friend of Wales and the world'. Paul Robeson understood that dignity, peace, justice and abundance were universal values to be available to all and he uniquely helped us to understand the indivisibility of those values.

For those who question his enduring legacy I need only refer to the Manic Street Preachers hymn of praise to him, 'Let Robeson Sing!' and its refrain, 'a voice so pure, a vision so clear' in 2001.

And, of course, the resonance of this wonderfully successful exhibition, 'Gadcwch i Paul Robeson Ganu!' which reminds older and younger generations in Wales of our shared values and our shared sacrifices.

Fel y dywedodd Paul Robeson yn 1953, mae e'n rhan o'n gwlad fach ni – pa wlad arall yn y byd all ddweud shwd beth?

As Paul Robeson said in 1953, he felt he was part of our small country – what other country in the world could make that claim?

14

The Fate of our Community: 'Iwerddon 1916, Rwsia 1917, Cymru?'
[Aberystwyth graffiti, 1978]*

I AM DOUBLY HONOURED TO give this lecture at the National Library of Wales which I first visited whilst at Gwersyll yr Urdd in Llangrannog in 1958. Our guide was the late Owen Edwards who was then working at the library. Circles really do intersect in Wales, in space and over time.

Firstly, I have long admired the admirable work of the Welsh Political Archive and recognise its remarkable holdings, not least those of the enigmatic Thomas Jones, variously described, somewhat jokingly by Baldwin as a 'bolshevik', by senior Whitehall civil servants as 'the little Welsh Socialist', by Michael Foot as 'an establishment flunky' and Aneurin Bevan rather bluntly as 'that old bugger from Rhymney'. Thomas Jones' 240 bound volumes and over 2,000 pages of small volumes, well over half a million words in length, are an incredible resource for contemporary historians.

---

* Text of the 24th Annual Welsh Political Archive Lecture, delivered at Y Drwm, National Library of Wales, 5 November 2010.

Secondly, I am honoured because I follow an impressive series of speakers, including my friends Dai Smith and Rhodri Morgan. Rhodri's only advice to me was 'dim copïo!'. Dai said, 'as always, be yourself'. I have taken their advice. So, here we go. It is Bonfire Night after all, so stand well back.

On 6 February 1979 I gave the funeral oration at an overflowing Abertridwr chapel to Jack Roberts, known locally and throughout the South Wales Valleys as 'Jack Russia'. Born in Penrhyndeudraeth, Merionethshire, appropriately as he said on May Day 1899, he described himself as a practising Christian and a practising Communist.

He was part of that great human wave of migrants who came south, worked at Senghennydd's Universal Colliery, was on the 'fortunate' shift in 1913 on that fateful day which took the lives of 439 miners; he became a Communist, was victimised for his union activities, imprisoned in the anti-scab Bedwas Riots in 1933, fought in 1937 in the International Brigades against Fascism in Spain; was secretary of the Workmen's Hall; and was chair of the Appeals Committee of the Caerphilly National Eisteddfod where Gwilym Tilsley won the Chair with 'Awdl Foliant i'r Glöwr'.

I said at his funeral:

> … a man like Jack Roberts, and all his comrades who went to Spain, has a special place within the Welsh Labour movement, and the whole of Welsh society …

Later that day I chaired a meeting in my home village of Creunant in the Dulais Valley in support of devolution in Wales. There seemed to be as many people on the platform as there were in the audience.

I was at the time a young extra-mural tutor, having just completed my doctoral thesis on Wales and the Spanish Civil War. I was a political activist and campaigner for devolution. I would have liked to describe myself – rather grandly – as the Irish poet and Labour politician Michael D. Higgins described Raymond Williams, as engaging in *praxis*, combining theoretical analysis with action, integrating our own personal biography with history:

> I welcomed [he said in his Raymond Williams Welsh Annual Lecture 'The Migrant's Return' in 1996] his commitment to a politics that opposed economic exploitation, cultural domination and personal repression through his practical involvement in the democratic work of university extension.

Michael D. Higgins is one of those rare 'organic intellectuals', not unlike Jack Roberts, who capture the mood of the times: they were, and are, the voices of our people, sometimes discordant, but nonetheless always authentic. Both, in their own ways, as Michael D. Higgins said of Raymond Williams, 'rendered the arid polarity between tradition and modernity redundant'.

I often reflect on that apparent paradox, why was it that so many people came to pay tribute to our collective past on 6 February 1979 and so few to find out about our own future? Jack spoke and lived *for us*: we spoke *at them*. Was the funeral, then, an affirmation of a commitment to a particular kind of common political culture and a particular kind of community? That is what I want to speak to you about tonight.

Choosing a title is always a challenge, particularly if what I have to say has diminished in contemporary and contextual relevance by the time the date arrives. Fortunately that is not so tonight. This title connects to our collective past, to our present, to our future, to Aberystwyth, and most of all to the work of one of Wales' great historians, my friend and my tutor, Emeritus Professor Ieuan Gwynedd Jones. I dedicate this lecture to him tonight and thank him for all that he has done in teaching generations of students, even though he told me that my writing was sometimes too *engagé*!

Of all the very distinguished Swansea historians who taught us in the 1960s – Glanmor Williams, Alun Davies, Ken Morgan, Prys Morgan, David Jones, Peter Stead – it was Ieuan who posed that very problematic question, 'what is distinctive about community in Wales?', a question repeated by that other great teacher and writer Raymond Williams, who, of course, described it as a slippery concept. I begin then with Ieuan's preface to his 1987 collection of essays on the social history of Victorian Wales entitled *Communities*:

> It is an illusion to believe that the processes by which communities were made in rural Wales were entirely different from those operating in industrial areas, as if the former was somehow insulated from the latter. Especially it is the relative simplicities of their social structures and their shared religious culture that needs to be stressed. It was these which made the transition from one to the other intelligible for the thousands of migrants who made the journey from country to town, and it was these which came to be expressed most completely and, for a time, most satisfyingly in *a common political culture* [my emphasis].

Ieuan's historically grounded phrase will be my personal and textual theme in this lecture.

In the late 1970s, when that Aberystwyth graffiti was painted, there was a millenarian, even for some an apocalyptic, feeling, very much a minority feeling as it turned out. It was a belief that Iwerddon 1916 and Rwsia 1917 would be followed by some revolutionary, evolutionary, awakening in 1979 in Wales, because we still believed that we shared, in Ieuan's words, 'a common political culture' which had existed in the recent past.

But to go beyond Ieuan's thesis to say that a common political culture existed in the 1970s as it had, say, in the 1870s, is to misrepresent the complexities of Welsh society over that time: as another of Ieuan's students, Dai Smith, has written, Wales is a 'plurality of cultures'. And we ignore them at our peril.

It is the task not just of politicians but of every active citizen to understand these complexities and not to assume that 'a common political culture' just happens, is always with us, is without a very specific definition, and can be conjured up by politicians, public servants and other opinion formers of various kinds who observe today's Wales – whenever they wish, through smoke and mirrors, to usher in the wish-fulfilment of unity.

Indeed, it is the task of every active citizen to understand not only what is meant by 'a common political culture', but what precisely is meant by 'community' and what is meant by 'nation'. So much of this is still what Michael D. Higgins called 'a reductive nostalgia', 'reactionary' and revealing a lack of genuine solidarity with 'the alleged bonds of parish and place'.

The artificial nineteenth-century construct of Wales defined, so often, as a nation by sobriety, sabbatarianism, the Welsh language and religious Nonconformity, would have excluded virtually everyone of us today and certainly Aneurin Bevan, Saunders Lewis and Shirley Bassey would not have had a welcome in those hillsides. I remember my late father enthusiastically coining the 1979 devolution slogan, 'Wales against the Tories'. It was, as it turned out, as inadequate and as divisive as Arthur Scargill's 'the miners united will never be defeated' in 1984–85. Both slogans presupposed 'a common political culture' and one 'community'. Both slogans were aspirational and well-meaning, but both were disconnected from political and social reality.

What did Ieuan mean by a common political culture? I think he meant a progressive, tolerant, enlightened, democratic culture, a virtual community that is simultaneously local, Welsh, British, European and global. It was both spiritual and secular. For me it is most emphatically the culture that has grown out of the

Enlightenment, it is the culture of Tom Paine, Richard Price, Robert Owen, Henry Richard, Eunice Stallard's Greenham Common, Tyrone O'Sullivan's Tower, and it is the culture too of our greatest honorary Welshman, Paul Robeson, who in 1957 implored us down that transatlantic telephone line to strive for those universal values of 'peace, dignity and abundance'.

That common political culture is, then, based on a community defined by the shared values of fellowship and social solidarity. But what does this all mean today and in the recent past? Is it the so-called 'fairness' of last month's (October 2010) Comprehensive Spending Review or is it the enduring and all-encompassing 'fairness' of the National Health Service, the nearest we have to a revered Constitution?

For me, it is, as ever, about political choices, or as Aneurin Bevan would have it, 'The religion of socialism is the language of priorities'. I remember being with Hywel Teifi Edwards the morning after the devolution vote in 1979. We were both angry and depressed; Hywel, as you would expect, more than me. And then two months later I was in the United States speaking to American miners who asked me about Margaret Thatcher. I said, rather foolishly, 'I don't know much about her, it doesn't matter anyway, she won't last'.

Let me move on to slightly firmer ground: my own family and community roots which most definitely shape my ideas about a common political culture and a Welsh and international community. For me, and for many of us, the personal is the political. It was a family and a community that were different, even 'odd', as Gwyn Alf described his own Dowlais: but it was definitely Welsh, even though inevitably it was like nowhere else.

Growing up in the mining community of Onllwyn in the Dulais Valley in a Christian-communist household there was obviously a mixture of influences. My father had himself been created by a mixture of influences: he learnt all his communication skills, as we call them now, in the chapel, including *canu penillion*, *adrodd*, *areithu*; at school he learnt to sing the 'Marseillaise' in Welsh through the influence of a progressive headteacher. His grandmother wanted him to be a *pregethwr*: his phenomenal memory of the Bible and of hymns would have stood him in good stead.

As it happens, that skill did prove useful occasionally in negotiating with employers and reaching out to the men and women he strove to represent; he was certainly, as we were, representative of a plurality of cultures and positions, personal and political.

On Sunday the communists cleaned the secular shrine, the Miners' Welfare Hall. I was one of them with my father. The rest of the day, *Ysgol Sul* and *Cwrdd* – I was one of those too, with my mother.

Our home welcomed such visitors as Krishna Menon, the future Indian Foreign Secretary, Cheddi Jagan, the future Prime Minister of Guyana, the Scottish historian Robin Page Arnot, and delegations of miners from China, the Soviet Union, Africa and many other countries. But we also welcomed the Reverend Erastus Jones and the Reverend Vivian Jones, the latter as a young minister who wished to understand the local community better by borrowing my father's copy of the *Communist Manifesto*.

In 1957 my father took me to hear Niclas y Glais, an old friend, preaching in nearby Rhigos and right on cue, as my father predicted, Niclas compared the new Soviet Sputnik with the star over Bethlehem. The local pit, too, was a microcosm of Wales and the world: there were Irish Catholics, free-thinking Spaniards, one of whom, Gregorio Esteban – whose brother Victoriano was killed in the International Brigades – taught Spanish through the medium of Welsh in Abercraf Welfare Hall. And there were even people from North Wales: my father was taught to sing with the harp by the chapel's *codwr canu*, Griffith Ellis Griffith from Caesarea near Caernarfon.

My father collected the Polish artist and Jewish refugee Josef Herman from Neath station and delivered him to Ystradgynlais, and then he appeared in nearby Cwmgïedd in the anti-Nazi film on the obliteration of the Czech village Lidice. *The Silent Village* is now seen as a masterwork of the great English documentary film maker, Humphrey Jennings. Sheltering a refugee came naturally to a Christian Socialist household whose ancestral roots stretched back to the Huguenots who had landed in Carmarthenshire several centuries before. All that was the unspoken but deeply-felt background to my family life before my own birth in 1946 into a Socialist Wales and a Socialist Britain.

In all this internationalism, there was to be no English spoken on the hearth until my sister married an Englishman in 1964. My father would admonish us, 'Beth yw'r Saesneg mawr hyn?'

My father's friends included Brinley and Tillie Griffiths. Brinley was a teacher and a conscientious objector of the First World War, and Tillie had been a suffragist: they counted amongst their friends Fenner Brockway, James Maxton, Sylvia Pankhurst and C. L. R. James who may have completed his monumental *Black Jacobins* in their home in Creunant. All were, in their different ways, world leaders, organic intellectuals, pioneers in the socialist, feminist and anti-colonial struggles – and all thankfully very engaged, very *engagé*.

One of Brinley's pupils was the writer Menna Gallie, who describes Brinley and the post-war world in her third novel, *The Small Mine* (1962):

> He was a kindly ageing socialist whose gods were Marx and Lenin, with Tolstoi to make up the Trinity and D. H. Lawrence as a seraph in close attendance. He was as bald as a monk with the face of a saint and patience to everlasting with kids …

He had the finest socialist library in South Wales – that was what attracted C. L. R. James in the 1930s. As a boy in the 1950s I would visit their home, called 'Camden' after Walt Whitman's home in New Jersey. He would say, 'Go to the library and choose a book'. The library had been bequeathed to the South Wales Miners' Federation and, before he died, we had already created the South Wales Miners' Library at University College Swansea. Professor Glanmor Williams said at the opening in 1973 that its creation out of the remnants of the old miners' institute libraries represented a modern affirmation of the purpose of the University of Wales, 'Prifysgol y Werin', 'the People's University'.

This was my first experience of a political assertion of the common political culture – it was an affirmation of Raymond Williams's 'Long Revolution' – that there is a common learning democratic culture which we all share, or at least we ought to be able to share. It was a community of shared values that we were embracing. It was at the same time dynamic, aspirational and permanently challenging. There was nothing romantic about any of this: but yes, it was idealistic about values and purpose even as it was both rooted and vulnerable.

This common political culture took on a particular form in the South Wales Valleys in the middle decades of the twentieth century. Admittedly this was exceptional in its distinctiveness. The people I have been describing – the last generation of largely self-educated men and women, Robespierre Thomas, Jim Kremlin and the Dai Dialectic of Menna Gallie's novels – were all organic intellectuals.

They were the antithesis of the opinion formers of today who allude to a common political culture which denies the conflicts of modern Welsh society: a society still divided by class, gender, race, language and disability. Together, all these constitute the 'Labour Question' which so baffled the Welsh Establishment of the early twentieth century, which in turn worried about the consequences of the apparently final progressive advances of the Chartist, Trade Union, Labour and Suffragette movements.

Political commentators today write frequently of the power of 'think tanks' on Government policy formulation. In the last hundred years I would suggest the most perceptive – although certainly by no means always correct – early think tank formulator was Thomas Jones, founder of Coleg Harlech, the Pilgrim Trust, *The Welsh Outlook*, Gregynog and all it represented.

It was in *The Welsh Outlook* that, revealingly, 'The Mind of the Miner' was explored in an anonymous article at the height of the Great War in July 1916:

> … The South Wales miner is a Celt and his Celtic fire and enthusiasm came into the fight with earnestness and vigour … The Welshman loves a strike like an Irishman loves a row …

It was Thomas Jones, confidante of prime ministers, caustically judged by Michael Foot as an 'Establishment flunky', friend of coal-owners, frequent visitor to Cliveden and alleged supporter of inter-war appeasement, who understood all too well that the Liberal hegemony in Wales had come to an end, even though he continued to serve anti-Labour coalitions.

In 1934, at Treharris Workmen's and Tradesmen's Library, he said:

> The story of the revolution is told on the shelves of your library. Compare the books you were buying and reading in 1884 and 1934. Today there are strange authors and strange subjects …
>
> Spengler's *Decline of the West*, Havelock Ellis, *Studies of the Psychology of the West* (6 vols), Bertrand Russell, *Marriage and Morals*, Bukharin, *Historical Materialism* …
>
> You have moved from Palestine to Russia. This is far less true of the books on the Welsh [language] shelves. There you have moved from volumes of sermons to volumes of stories and short

light essays. … It is a movement from theology to history and to fiction and shows very little trace of the volcanic eruptions which have thrown up the books on the English shelves.

What Thomas Jones had recognised was the battle of ideas between the Welsh Establishment's *The Welsh Outlook* and Keir Hardie's *Merthyr Pioneer*, and the triumph of the latter.

In scrolling forward nearly a century, I hesitate to suggest that the same battle may be taking place symbolically between Wales' two current think tanks, the Institute of Welsh Affairs and the Bevan Foundation. I could not possibly comment, because I am associated with one and not the other. But I can trace the lineaments, historical and cultural, that still inform divergent political opinions and actions.

And I do ask the central and pertinent question: are our think tanks and our universities connecting to the daily lives of the people of Wales and at the same time locating Wales within a wider world? Anyway, what is not in doubt is that the battle over the definition of that 'common political culture' and what we mean by 'community' continues today in its significance and importance as it did in Thomas Jones' time. There are many more self-styled opinion formers today, but none with TJ's gravitas, however flawed his judgement might have been.

That generation of organic intellectuals of the coalfield, of which my parents were a part, seized that ideological hegemony in 1945 and shaped their own distinct common political culture and sense of 'community'. It was that special kind of political culture in Wales and Britain that I took into my work simultaneously as an adult education tutor, political activist and historian. The creation of the South Wales Miners' Library out of the remnants of the workmen's institute libraries was the starting point in the early 1970s, along with the emergence of Llafur, what we then called the Welsh Labour History Society.

Dai Smith, in his review of my book on the miners' strike of

1984–85, *History on our Side* (2009), described me as 'historian as witness and activist as historian'. Fanciful or not, that is how I would characterise myself during this period, both at the university and maybe still in my parliamentary work.

Learning from the defeat of 1979 and the narrow slogan, 'Wales against the Tories', the Wales Congress in Support of Mining Communities during the miners' strike of 1984–85 was a political and historical affirmation of the need to build a common political culture based on shared community values.

Raymond Williams observed at the time in his essay, 'Mining the Meaning', that the common usage of such words as 'community' was testimony to a different and distinct culture. He signalled the coming of a 'new order'. We all held our breath. But a shift was taking place, connections were being made, again.

'Wales against the Tories' of 1979 had been superseded in 1984–85 by 'the NUM Fights for Wales' and Cymdeithas yr Iaith Gymraeg's 'Cau Pwll, Lladd Cymuned' and 'Heb Waith, Dim Iaith': such new slogans were testimony to that significant shift. Thus we had the range of diverse organisations, from Cymdeithas yr Iaith, to the Welsh Council of Churches and the gays and lesbians groups and everything else seemingly along the way, including sometimes parts of the police and the NCB management. It was a gramscian historic compromise which encircled and isolated, albeit briefly, the Conservative Government in Wales. Aberystwyth twinned with Maesteg, Rhiwbina with Rhondda Fach, Ynys Môn with Onllwyn, Blaenau Ffestiniog with Gwaun-Cae-Gurwen and Ystradgynlais with Nicaragua (I am still trying to work that one out).

But the inescapable fact was that we all had to re-adjust to what was soon a largely post-coal world in Wales. The next century, the one we are now in, would be different from both the two preceding ones, economically and socially. Culturally and politically, there were links to be made, and causes still to be served.

The creation of the Community University of the Valleys in 1993 – still prospering in nearly twenty locations in South-West Wales in 2010 – was one manifestation of this recurring common political culture, based here on collectivist learning, democratic partnerships between Swansea University and local communities which sought to preserve and enhance collectivist community values of social solidarity in a new post-coal era. There were others. And clarity of thought allied to the passion of commitment was still at the necessary core. We did not retreat from that. We built, again, on the lessons of history.

It is my belief that the shift in political thinking from the miners' strike onwards was a major, if not the major, contributing factor in the devolution victory of 1997, and this essentially is the central argument of my book on the strike, *History on our Side* (2009).

Now sometimes I would be challenged, and people would say that not everyone believes these political and historical assertions. But, you know, I take my inspiration from Iolo Morganwg, Dr William Price, Hywel Teifi Edwards and Gwyn Alf Williams. A quartet that would give the Marx Brothers a run for their money! I suspect they would agree with me that even if it isn't true, it deserves to be true.

In my parliamentary life since 2001, I have worked on the basis that we need to achieve a benign, caring element to our aspirational common political culture. My Carers (Equal Opportunities) Act in 2004 was based on the need to recognise that all carers should have the same equal opportunities as everyone else in society. And as the chair of the Welsh Affairs Committee in the last parliament, I worked always on the basis that we were the collective voice of Wales within parliament: so much so that when we achieved the impossible by publishing a unanimous report on the Welsh Language Legislative Competence Order, it was based on the genuine belief that all the main political parties in Wales had made their constructive contributions to the enhancing of the Welsh language. It is not true that I closed my eyes when I was speaking to the ranks of Welsh Tories, and imagined I was speaking only to the maverick simpatico Sir Wyn Roberts, later Lord Roberts of Conwy.

The Carers Act and the work of the Welsh Affairs Committee were a practical affirmation for me of the progressive universal values of the twentieth century – the values of figures as disparate and connected as David Lloyd George, Sir William Beveridge, Eleanor Rathbone, Aneurin Bevan, Jim Griffiths and Barbara Castle.

In my later role as chair of the Joint Committee on Human Rights I will obviously be championing the rights of all citizens, by defending the Human Rights Act and the Equality Act. That common political culture I have been talking about tonight is exemplified in these two pieces of legislation, standing as they do on the crucial building blocks of universality: the Welfare State, the Equal Pay Act – so eloquently illustrated in the film *Made in Dagenham* – and by the advances made in democratic devolution across the United Kingdom.

The Equalities and Human Rights Commission report, *How Fair is Britain?*, highlights deep racial, gender and class divisions in British society. If the Comprehensive Spending Review and any new legislation makes the situation worse, then my Joint Committee on Human Rights is duty-bound to hold the Government to account, particularly if vulnerable groups are put more at risk and fairness is denied.

When my father took me in 1964 to the all-night vigil in Llandaff Cathedral organised to save the lives of Nelson Mandela, Walter Sisulu and the other brave comrades of the African National Congress following the Rivonia Trial, we were all affirming our common universal political culture and our belief in a shared community of values, of fellowship, of social solidarity and co-operation or, as I said earlier, as Paul Robeson put it, 'peace, dignity and abundance'. Recently, some of us voted for a new leader of the Labour Party. Interestingly, Ed Miliband talked about the 'personal being the political', as I have done tonight. He used one word towards the end of his speech which had a particular resonance for me. He used the word 'optimist'. I thought he was in good company. I remember Gwyn Alf quoting the Italian Marxist Antonio Gramsci quoting, I believe, the French Socialist Romain Rolland, 'pessimism of the intellect, optimism of the will'. I remember too my friend and fellow adult education tutor, the Welsh writer Alun Richards, being asked by a nurse, 'What is your religion?' He simply replied, 'Just put down optimist'.

The re-emergence of the historically important Welsh parliamentary party is another sign of optimism in response to the growing feeling that we need a cross-party forum in Westminster to fight for fairness for the people of Wales. A creation of the era of *Cymru Fydd*, it may well once again make a benign contribution towards strengthening our common political culture. We should recognise all of this, and more, as we move towards the possibility of a stronger National Assembly in 2011. At the moment, that referendum vote is being eclipsed in importance by the attack on the public sector upon which our communities and our common political culture are crucially built.

We will, of course, need more than just 'optimism' in the coming political struggle following the Comprehensive Spending Review, which will require resistance within Wales and far beyond Wales. A bold start has been made, thanks to devolution, with the joint statement of the First Ministers of the three devolved administrations. But 'optimism' is a good starting point. The 'ladies' of Dagenham and their sisters in Merthyr remind us that whatever those who presume to speak for us may say, a common political culture must be based on consent. And to get there we must be willing to dissent from those who set out to speak for Wales by conveniently forgetting the Welsh people on the ground.

I discussed earlier Thomas Jones's presumption to 'understand' Wales. Today there are many more TJs populating our Welsh Establishment and far more 'National Institutions' presuming to speak for Wales far beyond our own democratically elected National Assembly for Wales.

I was recently in the Appalachian Mountains in the United States, where the struggle for economic, political and environmental justice parallels that in Wales. The danger in both places however is *introspection*, in our case, specifically and exclusively on constitutional matters. Whether it is BBC Wales, the Church in Wales, the Institute of Welsh Affairs or *The Western Mail* – they all in their different ways have been giving, *until recently*, high prominence to constitutional matters.

I say 'until recently' with some deliberation, because I detect a sea change. Archbishop Barry Morgan's championing of the poor in Wales gives us great hope; his is the authentic and progressive voice of Wales and his decisive intervention, as ever, is to be welcomed. Now, whether that perspective continues in the coming months and whether the Welsh people will agree with their self-appointed opinion leaders, only time will tell. For those of us who will support the Yes Campaign in 2011 for enhanced powers for the Assembly, the challenge is a considerable one. Unless we connect the constitutional question to the daily lives of ordinary people and their jobs and their public services, then we deserve to lose. Political justice must be accompanied by social and economic justice.

So, any constitutional change will require the enthusiastic endorsement of Wales's great estates. Not the landed estates of the eighteenth century, but the working-class housing estates of

Penparcau, Penrhys, Gurnos and Sandfields, whose working-class families are under threat today from the present Coalition Government's Comprehensive Spending Review. My guess is that their democratic voices will be heard and *they* will determine our fate now that our common political culture is threatened. It will be a case then of 'tynged ein cymuned', 'the fate of our community', which is the real title of this lecture.

As Thomas Jones said perceptively again, and writing of his own time of working for the reactionary coalitions of his own day, and this may be a warning to all those who aspire to speak from such a position for Wales or Britain:

> I have lived too long among the miners and steelworkers of South Wales to fail to remind my masters that politics are concerned with the lives of ordinary folk.

Gyfeillion, comrades and friends, they may have been *his* masters, but they have never been mine! Nor will they be Wales's, so long as that common political culture continues to be a wellspring for all of us into the future, as it has been in our past and should be today.

III

Bread and Roses!

15

'Sam's Bill': 'The Right to an Ordinary Life'*

IN JULY 2004 THE Carers (Equal Opportunities) Bill passed through its last stage in Parliament when my friend, Lord Jack Ashley of Stoke, the redoubtable champion of people with disabilities, uttered at the third and final Reading in the Lords the words, 'that this Bill be now passed'. Lord Ashley, who took the Bill through the Lords, was my most important ally. His total commitment is summed up in the words which he wrote in *The House,* Parliament's magazine:

> Carers quite simply need caring for … Many of them do not even claim their entitlements because they are unaware of them. The new bill will ensure that they are systematically given information, that their health is considered by the social services and health departments and that they get new opportunities for education, training and employment. It can change the lives of millions of harassed people.

I am pleased to be recalling this achievement here in the South Wales Valleys because we have a disproportionate number

---

* Text of the fourth Annual Bevan Foundation Lecture delivered in Tredegar on 16 July 2005 and published by the Foundation as a pamphlet entitled *The Right to an Ordinary Life: Carers and Equal Opportunities.*

of carers, despite the advances achieved by Aneurin Bevan's National Health Service. Carers provide freely the equivalent of £57 billion, which is about the cost of the NHS.

This paper is about the campaign to achieve equal rights for carers, what we came to call in the course of that campaign, 'the right to an ordinary life' and 'Sam's Bill'. The paper is also about what has been achieved since the passing of what became the Carers (Equal Opportunities) Act 2004 and what still needs to be done.

Why a Carers (Equal Opportunities) Act?

Why then do we need a Carers (Equal Opportunities) Act? The national *advocacy* body for carers, Carers UK, defines carers in this way:

> Carers look after family, partners or friends in need of help because they are ill, frail or have a disability. The care they provide is unpaid. Almost all of us have been or will be a carer during our lifetime.

In 1980 my wife Mair and I became carers of our son Sam, who had Down's syndrome. Throughout the period we were carers, until he died in May 1997, we were unaware of the term, although we were active members of a carers' organisation, the Down's Syndrome Association. It is only with the passing of two Private Members' Bills for carers, the growing impact of campaigning by carers' organisations, the identification of 5.2 million carers through the 2001 census and finally the Labour Government's launch of its National Strategy for Carers in 1999, that the scale and nature of the plight facing carers has begun to be appreciated. The actual figure of 5.2 million carers has subsequently been revised upwards and has been calculated at between 6 million and 7 million. This amounts to at least 12 per cent of the adult population.

The headline statistics are startling. In any year, 301,000 adults in the UK become carers. Over a lifetime, seven out of ten women will be carers. Women are 25 per cent more likely to become carers than men. Three out of five carers have had to give up work to become carers, and there are 175,000 young carers under the age of eighteen and 945,000 are aged over sixty-five. Perhaps most shocking of all, carers are calculated to be twice as likely to suffer poor health as non-carers.

In Wales, there are 350,000 carers, of whom over 20,000 are in Neath Port Talbot, which represents the highest proportion of carers per head of population in the whole of the UK. The county also has the highest proportion of heavy end carers (those caring for over fifty hours a week).

All of this is a legacy of our industrial past. It is not unconnected to the causes of the health inequalities in the Valleys of South Wales and other post-industrial regions of the UK. I have always believed that the personal is the political. That is why my Maiden Speech on 25 June 2001 was on people with disabilities and their carers, which I described as an essential journey of hope from social inclusion to social justice. My objective then was summed up in these words and it remains so in this paper:

> In my first speech to the House, I want to focus specifically on the citizenship rights of disabled people and their carers in relation to the economy and to the whole of society. Our new Labour Government should and will be measured by the extent to which we tackle, in partnership, the fundamental inequalities faced by disabled people and their carers.

Two previous Private Members' Bills made some significant progress for carers. The Carers (Recognition and Services) Act 1995, introduced by Malcolm Wicks MP, gave a right to a separate assessment for people providing informal care. The Carers and

Disabled Children's Act 2000 introduced by Tom (now Lord) Pendry gave carers enhanced rights of assessment.

Nevertheless, the take-up of carers' assessments was very patchy across the country. The plight of carers was still one largely of isolation, being besieged and undervalued. Carers were still denied equal opportunities. Their lives, beyond their caring responsibilities, were still not recognized.

Seizing the time!

My maiden speech had focused on this question of social justice and that feeling was rooted in the reality of Mair and me caring for our son Sam. On 4 December 2003 I came second in the Private Members' Bill ballot. The choice of subject was already made. It was Mair who said within the family, 'this is Sam's Bill'. From then 'Sam's Bill' became part of what has been called a 'carers' movement'.

The day after the ballot I wrote in my diary:

This is National Carers' Rights Day. Visited Brynhyfryd Primary School. Then onto CVS for carers/enablers meeting. Turning point. Gaynor Richards of (CVS), Lynn Coleman and two young mothers – all very impressive. We worked on a carers' charter in which lifelong learning a vital dimension. I began to think about a carers' bill along those lines …

That meeting encapsulated what the Bill set out to achieve: 'the right to an ordinary life', which were the words of one of the carers I met on that day.

The parliamentary launch on 26 January included carers from all parts of the country, the Mayor from my County Borough, Councillor Peter Lloyd and two Health Ministers, Stephen Ladyman for England and Jane Hutt for Wales.

The broad cross-party support in the two Houses of Parliament and the breadth of support outside Parliament from carers' organisations to educational bodies, the Equal Opportunities Commission, Local Government bodies in England and Wales, trades unions and employers, ensured the passing of the Bill, which received Royal Assent on 22 July 2004, the very last day before the summer recess. My Bill team included leading members of all the main parties (Conservative, Labour and Liberal Democrat) along with representatives from Plaid Cymru and the Ulster Unionists. This breadth of support was mirrored in the Lords, with all parties again prominent, along with crossbenchers Baroness Howe and Lord Rix (President of Mencap) very prominent.

My own union, Community (at the time ISTC), was typical of the extra-parliamentary backing at every stage of the Bill's progress. Its journal, *ISTC Today*, proclaimed in a double-page spread, 'A carers' journey of hope: How new legislation sponsored by ISTC and Labour MP Mr Hywel Francis could offer carers new opportunities to build lives beyond their caring responsibilities'.

The significant national and local media interest in the Bill's progress has, according to Carers UK, played a major role in raising awareness about carers' lives more generally and in ensuring public support. It was the strength of the Bill team and extra-parliamentary support which ensured that young carers were included in the legislation: initially the Government was not sympathetic to their inclusion.

The apparent ease of the passage of the Bill is misleading. From the outset, I took advice from experienced Parliamentarians and had the constant support of Carers UK, whose human rights lawyer, Luke Clement, helped draft the Bill. I was told I needed to meet three essential requirements to achieve success: gain the support of the Chancellor, win Government support and also cross-party support. All were equally important, and one big advantage was that the Prime Minister himself had always been supportive of carers. My first initiative was to speak to the Chancellor, Rt Hon. Gordon Brown MP, in the very first days. It was his words of encouragement and his advice to seek the support of Tom Clarke MP and Lord Ashley which proved crucial.

The purpose of the Carers (Equal Opportunities) Act 2004

This is an England and Wales Act. It required and achieved official Government support in England led by the then Carers' Minister in England, Stephen Ladyman, and the then Health Minister in Wales, Jane Hutt. Having been negotiated with ministers in both seats of power, it was truly a child of devolution. It also built on advances for carers which had been achieved by the devolved administrations in Northern Ireland and Scotland.

The purpose of the Act is to recognize that carers have 'the right to an ordinary life', an equal opportunity with others in society to access leisure, work, education and training beyond their caring responsibilities.

The Chief Executive of Carers UK, Imelda Redmond, has said that the very title of the Act has made a significant difference:

> … one of the most radical and far-reaching elements of the Act is the title. This has really helped bring about a culture shift, it has shifted people's mind sets from thinking they should be kind to these people to a rights based equality of opportunity. The change in language is noticeable to us.

The long title of the Act is 'an Act to place duties on local authorities and health bodies in respect of carers; and for connected purposes'. The principal aims of the Act are to:

ensure that work, lifelong learning and leisure are considered when a carer is assessed;

give local authorities new powers to enlist the help of housing, health, education and other local authorities in providing support to carers;

ensure that carers are informed of their rights.

Breathing life into the new Act

Shortly before the Bill entered the Statute Book, one of its key supporters, Tom Clarke, the Scottish Labour MP who had been the first Disability Minister in the 1997 Government, said to me, 'Don't let the Act gather dust on the shelf: we must breathe life into it.'

With that wise advice ringing in my ears, the Bill team which I had constructed in Westminster, along with supporters in the Welsh Assembly and carers' organisations throughout the country, set about organising celebrations which focused principally on plans for the future.

In Wales, within days of Royal Assent, the then Health Minister, Jane Hutt, announced an All Wales Carers' Summit. Held prior to the General Election, the delegates came forward with a range of radical proposals, including a Carers' Commissioner. Nearer home the leader of Neath Port Talbot County Borough Council, Councillor Derek Vaughan, and I held a meeting on 28 July involving professionals and carers, in order to run pilot schemes ahead of the implementation of the Act in April 2005. The result was a range of initiatives negotiated with carers. They included young parents' learning opportunities at SNAC, a local parent-led charity; life skills learning for young carers; informal courses for the local Alzheimer's Society; and a primary care initiative working with GPs to refer carers under stress on to learning and leisure opportunities, with guidance and support.

And most encouraging of all, a Carers Action Movement – the first in the UK – was launched in Neath Port Talbot during this year's carers' week. Led by carer Ray Thomas, it is a self-help organisation which stems from the desire to improve the welfare of carers locally. Facilitated by the body which hosted my carers' meeting in December 2003, Neath Port Talbot Council for Voluntary Service, the movement has already achieved the appointment of a Carers' Development Officer, and is pressing for the appointment of dedicated assessment officers (a role which already exists in Barnet).

At the UK level, the adult learners' body NIACE and Carers UK came together for the first time in a collaborative exercise to highlight lifelong learning opportunities for carers, with an excellent pamphlet entitled *Carers and Learning*. This was followed by a parallel publication in Wales, *Balancing Life and Caring*, produced by Carers Wales (which has also previously been published in England in a different form).

Then, shortly before the 2005 General Election, an All Party Parliamentary Group for Carers was established, to monitor progress on the implementation of the Act and to be an advocacy body for carers in Parliament, and to liaise with the devolved bodies in the UK and internationally. A parallel All Party Group was set up in the Welsh Assembly recently.

The Westminster All Party Group held its first seminar on the theme of lifelong learning, identifying good practice already developing in a number of educational bodies, including the Open University, the National Extension College and City & Guilds. And the Princess Royal Trust for Carers and the National Extension College are publishing their report, 'Making Learning Accessible to Unpaid Carers', a three-year distance learning project funded by the Big Lottery Fund. The Westminster All Party Group held further seminars on flexible working and women carers and pensions (following on from work by the

Equal Opportunities Commission and my former parliamentary colleague, Helen Jackson).

Alongside all these developments, there was the distinct campaign by the shop workers' union USDAW, 'Supporting Parents and Carers'. This latter initiative was the culmination of a wider trade union campaign for more support for parents and carers, including flexible work opportunities, and this was enshrined in the Trade Unions/Labour Party Warwick Agreement prior to the 2005 General Election.

The wider policy context

All these developments begged the question: What was the wider policy context? It was, of course, the transformation of the Welfare State through a new work-life balance, including the National Childcare Strategy: the principles which underpinned that strategy applied equally to carers. Many think tanks entered the debate, including the Fabian Society with its interim report on life chances and child poverty. In the specific area of carers, pioneering policy work by Barbara Keeley and Malcolm Clarke in 2003, on behalf of the Princess Royal Trust for Carers, raised awareness of the crucial questions of support and information, particularly amongst GPs and primary care professionals.

The Social Exclusion Unit (SEU) of the Office of the Deputy Prime Minister (ODPM) identified the key drivers of social exclusion as low income, education, ill health, housing, transport, social capital, neighbourhood, crime and the fear of crime.

In its review of the literature for the SEU in the Breaking the Cycle series, the ODPM correctly stated that:

> Social exclusion was also driven by policy issues … Policy is critical and we now benefit from it being driven by the social exclusion agenda with targets and monitoring …

For too long, carers have not been recognised as a socially

excluded group worthy of proper consideration and respect. That is now thankfully changing.

That invisibility in relation to policy development was being diminished as a consequence of two related initiatives. Firstly, the growing impact of the Action for Carers and Employment (ACE) Project will inevitably result in further recognition of carers' potential in the labour market and more widely in social policy. ACE National was a development partnership led by Carers UK and funded by the European Social Fund's Equal Programme. Its purpose was to raise awareness of the barriers facing carers who wished to work and to test and promote ways of supporting them.

Secondly, the research work undertaken on behalf of ACE National by Sheffield Hallam University had for the first time examined in detail the data on carers provided by the 2001 census. The future need for carers; the relationship between carers, employment and health; the relationship between carers and family responsibilities; and the geographical distribution of carers: all these major factors will have a significant impact on the planning of the NHS, on social services and on the voluntary sector. The recently published Green Paper on Social Care will be massively influenced by the detailed analysis of carers and their needs undertaken by Sheffield Hallam University. It should also be acknowledged that the Green Paper has been influenced by the Act: the acknowledgement of carers having a life beyond caring is seen as a significant driver in the vision for social care.

In an interview with *Contact*, the Carers Wales publication, Dr Brian Gibbons AM, the then Welsh Assembly Health Minister, stated that his key objectives for carers included:

> more general recognition that while many carers are service users, they are also a resource. Carers are part of the solution … carers' issues should not be regarded as an add-on to 'mainstream' services but should become an integral part of the planning process.

Carers are undeniably a resource. This Act recognizes them as human beings too.

With that in mind I worked with the Bevan Foundation, other MPs, local authorities and most of all with carers, to identify ways in which my Carers (Equal Opportunities) Act would be implemented at community level involving former carers as key drivers of policy change, emphasizing active lives rather than economic inactivity. This would build on the Bevan Foundation's report, *Ambitions for the Future*, published in 2003.

My experience in different parts of the UK during National Carers' Week in 2005, from Swansea to Sunderland and from Port Talbot to Barnet, was that there was a perceptible attitudinal shift, with carers moving from the shadows to centre stage in policy and practice. But we have a long way to go before carers win 'the right to an ordinary life'.

16

Remembering Richard Burton[*]

MAE'N ANRHYDEDD I NI i gyd fod yma heddiw gyda theulu a ffrindiau yr anfarwol Richard Burton. Mae'n anrhydedd personol i mi, fel Aelod Seneddol Aberafan, etholaeth oedd yn cynnwys y cyfan o Bontrhydyfen pan gafodd Richard ei eni.

It is a privilege to be here today with family and friends to recognise the life of Richard Burton at Pontrhydyfen where he was born in 1925. At that time the whole of Pontrhydyfen was in the Aberavon constituency. My neighbouring Member of Parliament, Peter Hain, sends his very good wishes and warmly welcomes this Trail as I do.

Richard's niece, Sian Owen, and I have been asked to say something about 'remembering Richard Burton'. It has been said, and we all agree, that his was the greatest voice of the English language. If somehow we forget everything else, it is the voice of Richard Burton that is immortal – mae ei lais yn anfarwol.

As a sign of that immortality, one of our grandsons, Evan,

---

[*] Text of a speech on the occasion of the opening of the Richard Burton Trail, Pontrhydyfen, 10 June 2011.

has convinced his brothers, Elis and Aled, and his cousins David, Elena and Efa, that Richard's narration of *The War of the Worlds* is awesome. For me, what is equally significant is the fact that as a child growing up in the South Wales Valleys in the post-war world, it was he who represented that sense of hope and confidence of a new generation and a new world.

A new world was being created and he was helping to create it. He was for all of us children 'the Aneurin Bevan of stage and screen'. Aneurin Bevan gave the world the first National Health Service. And Richard Burton was, for us, and many across the world, the greatest film star and greatest actor of his generation, and he was one of us.

He and Aneurin Bevan were both sons of South Wales miners, and they represented in their different ways a creative and powerful force. And when they spoke, they were unmistakably Welsh and you felt they spoke for us. I remember being taken – indeed queuing – to see *The Robe* in the early 1950s. It was in Seven Sisters Miners' Welfare Cinema. What was most important of all was that he was a product of our mining communities, and we were proud of him and his achievements. And in turn, Richard Burton always showed that he was proud of *his* roots and *his* origins.

This Trail, then, reminds us of Richard's origins. And we stand here at the Miners' Arms where Richard was interviewed by Vincent Kane of the BBC in 1977. In that interview he talked of the profound family, community and educational values and influences on his life. Afterwards, Vincent Kane said he had never felt so enriched by the experience of such an interview.

Richard's widow, Sally – who has done so much to perpetuate his memory – sends her warmest wishes to everyone here today and a special thanks to those who have brought this Trail to fruition. It is a delight to see that one of those who have played a big part in bringing about this Trail, and who is with us today – Dick Wagstaffe – has been honoured with an MBE in today's Queen's Birthday Honours List.

I have also received a message from Kate, Richard's daughter, who said this:

> Please say that I wish I could be there and cannot wait to walk the Trail as I love to walk and hike, just like my father!

In the many discussions I have had with Sally and Graham about the way we commemorate Richard's life, we all agreed that it should be lasting and of educational value. That is why we have established this Trail, the Annual Richard Burton Lecture – this year it is on 4 October in Port Talbot's Princess Royal Theatre.

And that is why we also have the Richard Burton Archives and the Richard Burton Research Centre at Swansea University; the Portrait Bench and the 10K Race at Cwmafan; as well as the dedicated room in the Afan Lodge Hotel. In remembering Richard Burton, we are doing so in a purposeful way, using his legacy to look forward.

I am confident that there will be many more local ways to commemorate Wales' greatest actor, a proud son of Pontrhydyfen and Taibach, and no doubt we could say a proud son of Cwmafan as well. After *The Night of the Iguana* everyone from Tonmawr would have a claim too. We may well need to extend the Trail to include these other communities, including Dyffryn Rhondda where Richard and Graham performed in Eisteddfodau and where their father worked in the colliery.

As the chair of the Richard Burton Advisory Board and the Member of Parliament for Aberavon, I promise you that the new relationship between Neath Port Talbot County Borough Council and Swansea University will have at its heart an ever-growing recognition of the contemporary relevance of Richard Burton for succeeding generations of young people from our local communities – and for the many visitors from all over the world who come to learn about Richard's proud origins here in the Afan Valley.

Mwynhewch y daith a'r atgofion!

Enjoy the walk and the memories!

17

'Joe Bach'
and the Holocaust*

Today [12 January 2012] is Holocaust Memorial Day, when we pledge to challenge the language of hatred, give voice to the voiceless, and work to create a society free from persecution and hatred.

Whenever I think of the Holocaust I think of Josef Herman, Lidice and Ystradgynlais. The full scale and horror of the Holocaust cannot begin to be understood until we look at the individual lives and individual communities which were destroyed across Europe and across the world.

I was brought up in the post-war period surrounded by mining communities which had played their full part in defeating the advance of Nazism and fascism. Near to us was Ystradgynlais which had a unique place in that struggle. In 1942–43 a film, *The Silent Village*, was made there, depicting the Nazi obliteration of the Czech mining village of Lidice, where all the men were executed and all the women and children sent to concentration camps.

Two years later the artist Josef Herman arrived in Ystradgynlais. I am proud to say that there is a belief in our family that my late father brought him from Neath railway station. 'Joe Bach', as he

---

* Text of a blog written on 12 January 2012 for The Bevan Foundation.

quickly became known in the locality, had fled Poland because of the rise of anti-Semitism across Europe. His life in Wales is told in a very moving exhibition currently at Swansea County Hall.

Josef Herman stayed in Wales for eleven years, and like another great artist driven from his country by intolerance, Paul Robeson, he is for us a true Welshman, a citizen of our country. We welcomed and embraced them both. During his life in Ystradgynlais Josef Herman depicted on canvas the life of a Welsh mining community in his unique, distinctively sombre yet very human way.

The true measure of his achievement in this period was in 1951, when he was commissioned by the organisers of the Festival of Britain to produce a mural which he called *Miners*. This is one of the great artistic treasures of Wales, now located at the Glynn Vivian Art Gallery in Swansea.

As an artist he influenced many artists locally and internationally, including my friend the Treforgan miner, the late Cyril Ifold, some of whose work hangs in the South Wales Miners' Library. Cyril also designed the local Ynyscedwyn miners' banner which celebrates the universal values of music and social solidarity.

Today his influence endures through the inspirational work of the Ystradgynlais-based Josef Herman Art Foundation Cymru, which does sterling work in encouraging local children to engage in artistic work, and in so doing become aware of the talent and courage of one of the survivors of the Holocaust. I am proud to be one of its patrons.

How many good decent people like Josef Herman perished because of the Holocaust? In Wales, we remember them all through the life and work of Josef Herman, 'Joe Bach' of Ystradgynlais.

18

London and the Miners' Strikes of the Twentieth Century*

IT IS A PRIVILEGE and a delight to be invited to speak tonight to the Cymmrodorion and Wales in London. In thinking about what I should say I was reminded of that warning to all governments of the twentieth century: there are two bodies you take on at your peril – the Brigade of Guards and the Miners' Union. I am often asked in the House of Commons by Conservative members when they see my red and black Aberavon RFC Wizards tie, 'I didn't know you were in the Guards?' What they would do if I also wore my father's South Wales Miners' Saltley Gates 1972 commemorative tie … give me a wide berth I guess.

Forty years ago this month my wife and I and our one-month-old daughter Hannah were in the Hayward Gallery next to the Royal Festival Hall to see the Arts Council Exhibition entitled *Art in Revolution*. One of the volunteer attendants, a very elderly Cockney, told us he had been to Wales only once, to a place called Tonypandy in 1910 or 1911. He had been one of Churchill's

---

* A lecture given to the Honourable Society of Cymmrodorion (in association with Wales in London) on 16 March 2011, and published in the *Transactions of the Honourable Society of Cymmrodorion*, New Series, Vol. 18, 2012.

troops. We were living in London, in 'Welsh' Ealing, because I was working at the TUC. I was still there a year later during the memorable and indeed successful miners' strike of 1972. I was witness in a small way to those historic events both nationally and locally in Ealing and in the South Wales Valleys.

I begin in this very personal way, because as a contemporary historian – albeit somewhat lapsed nowadays – and as a politician, I believe that the personal is the political. I want to share some of my own memories and what oral historians call received memories.

The received memories relate a great deal to my late father, Dai Francis, who was the general secretary of the National Union of Mineworkers in South Wales between 1963 and 1976 and the founding chair of the Wales TUC in 1975. His working life began and ended with the starkly contrasting great strikes of the 1920s and the 1970s. He had an overwhelming sense that the latter were a vindication of the former. When he was born in 1911, there were nearly one million miners in Britain – a quarter of them in South Wales. When he retired in 1976 there were still a quarter of a million. Now, in 2012, there are barely ten thousand.

London figures in the drama of the great miners' strikes and lockouts of the last century because it was the seat of political power, and for the first half of the century it was the seat of imperial power. Even though the coal industry appeared decentralised, at least in terms of ownership and in a geographical and cultural sense, real political power was centralised here in London, in Westminster and Whitehall, and to an extent at the TUC and through the main national political parties. And the enlightened Welsh miners' leaders who came to lead the British miners during crucial periods in the last century knew that too.

General secretaries of the national union, all from South

Wales – Frank Hodges (1918–24), Arthur Cook (1924–31), Arthur Horner (1946–58) and Will Paynter (1959–68) – knew the importance of being near the seat power by ensuring that the union's headquarters was here in London. By striking contrast, in its hour of greatest need, the NUM was led into oblivion by Arthur Scargill when he removed the union headquarters to Yorkshire on the eve of the last great strike of 1984–85: I will say more of that later. Whilst Cardiff was the greatest coal metropolis in the world in the early decades of the twentieth century, it was always acknowledged that it was to London we had to turn to resolve the great problems of the industry and our mining communities – working conditions, wages, health and education, even the ownership of the industry. Negotiations with employers, with Government, the lobbying of Parliament and the passing of legislation, solidarity from other unions, were all to be sought here in London. Cardiff in that sense was not at all important. A strange illustration of this was my father, who came to London as a child in 1924 to the Great Wembley Exhibition but never went to Cardiff until his wedding day in 1936.

To begin at the beginning, for our mining communities in the anthracite coalfields of south-west Wales, the riotous 'Ammanford' strike of 1925 seemed historically to loom larger than even 1926. Fifty-nine miners were imprisoned. The released prisoners and their families participated in London rallies, and there were representations to the Home Office for early release, led by the TUC. At a protest rally in March 1926 in the Royal Albert Hall, over 10,000 people assembled and heard Tom Dafen Williams, a recently released Ammanford prisoner, address them. The previous month, a petition of 300,000 signatures was presented to Parliament for the release of these imprisoned anthracite miners. But the whole decade for the miners, indeed for the whole British trade union movement, was dominated by the 1926 General Strike and the seven-month miners' lockout.

There had been major strikes and lockouts earlier in the century which had had national significance: the 1910–11 Cambrian lockout and Tonypandy riots, the 1912 National Minimum Wage Strike, the 1915 South Wales Strike which threatened the war effort – and Lloyd George as Minister of Munitions for once came down to Cardiff to settle the dispute. And then there was the threat of a national strike to nationalise the industry in 1919 and the bitter three-month National Lockout of 1921. But none of these conflicts compared with 1926. As if to illustrate the plight of Wales and its mining communities, Dewi Emrys, the Crown bard at the 1926 Swansea National Eisteddfod, pawned his Crown – it was found in a London pawn shop.

We often wrongly attribute to the miners' strike of 1984–85 some belated feminist awakening in the coalfields. On the contrary, a cursory study of 1926 would reveal not only women organising the food kitchens – obviously a natural extension of their domestic role – but also leading riots and demonstrations across the coalfields to stem the tide back to work. In a remarkable study entitled *Women and the Miners' Lockout*, Marion Phillips, the chief woman officer of the Labour Party, described the women's political role through the Women's Committee for the Relief of the Miners and Children. Whilst campaigning occurred throughout the country and indeed internationally, the centre of activity was London, with frequent visits of Welsh male voice choirs from the Valleys – a kind of early version of the 1,000 voices! In one weekend, miners' choirs raised £250, ranging from a £70 collection in Letchworth Village Hall to an audience of very poor people at St George's Hall in the Old Kent Road, where Miss Ellen Wilkinson collected £10. Walter Peacock, Secretary to the Duchy of Cornwall, sent £10 from the Prince of Wales. In his letter he said:

> HRH necessarily cannot take sides in any dispute; but we all owe
> a debt to the miners in the past, and everyone feels sympathy for
> their wives and children in their hour of distress.

Marion Phillips recalled that Welsh choirs went abroad. One
went to Russia; the Blaina Cymric Choir sang at factories, public
meetings and concert halls. Miners' wives accompanied choirs to
London as the main speakers, relating their personal experiences.
At one women's meeting in the Kingsway Hall, chaired by
Margaret Bondfield, the actress Sybil Thorndike spoke alongside
five miners' wives. These wider social and cultural dimensions
were to be repeated six decades later, particularly in London.

Despite defeat, despite a sense of betrayal, despite everything,
London was a very special place for miners. It might have had
an alien government, but it was a place of sustenance, a place
to seek work, a place of solidarity, and dare we say it, it was
a place of at least occasional pleasure and enjoyment, it was a
kind of second home (without the scrutiny of chapel deacons),
with so many ex-patriot Welsh there with a helping hand, as
we found, again, when we came two generations later. We
knew our way around, maybe through families removed there
during the Depression, or because of Twickenham. 'Follow
me boys,' one miner lobbying the NUM leadership in 1981
said, 'I know the way to Soho.' He actually said, 'Solo'. And
in 1984, Long Tom Jones, a retired miner, wanted to fundraise
in London because 'these Bohemian feminists in Belgravia
appreciate the good intellectual conversation of Welsh miners,'
as he put it.

By the time the 1972 national miners' strike occurred, I had
already been working for the TUC for nearly a year. Mair and
I helped organise the billeting of Kent miners across the city;
Mair went with our daughter Hannah to provide food for the
pickets at West Drayton power station. I was privileged to hear
the miners' leader, Lawrence Daly, address the closed session of

the General Council of the TUC. In that quiet, cultured, lilting Fife voice he made two modest requests: 'don't cross our picket lines and organise a transport workers' conference.'

On the first day of the strike, I went, with other TUC staff, up to the headquarters of the union in Euston Road. The building was being run by Kent miners and Lawrence was around the corner in his favourite pub. The strike was running itself, out in the coalfields. Lawrence had sent out a circular to all NUM branches. The tone was simple: no violence, only peaceful picketing, behave as ambassadors of your communities.

I was home in Cardiff one weekend early on in the strike. Activists from the rail unions came to see my father on a Sunday morning and told him where to place pickets to stop all coal movements. Within days there were no coal movements at all across Britain. Every week my father stayed with us in our small flat in Ealing. He slept on the 'studio couch' and did interviews for BBC Radio Wales early in the morning on the progress of the strike on our neighbour's telephone.

The Wales-England game at Twickenham had a special quality. A striking miner, Dai Morris of Tower, was in the victorious Welsh side. My father was convinced that it was divine intervention on behalf of the Welsh miners. Many years later, just weeks before my father died in 1981, he had a lift to the Wales-England game at the National Stadium with the Mayor of Rhymney. As he got out of the mayoral car who should be getting out of the nearby car of Alun Priday, secretary of Cardiff Rugby Club, but former Prime Minister Edward Heath. My father introduced himself, explaining that they last met in Downing Street during the miners' strike of 1972. My father simply said: 'We beat you then in 1972. We beat you last week – [Margaret Thatcher had done her now forgotten U-turn on pit closures] and we'll beat you again today!'

We get a flavour of those times too when we read the evidence of the Wilberforce Inquiry which came down on the side of the miners. Take one witness from South Wales:

> My name is Alan Carter, I am thirty-three years old; I am married with four children. I work in Mardy Colliery in the Rhondda Valley in South Wales. I am a surface Grade 2 worker doing jobs which include driving a diesel loco, a Coles crane, and a sixteen-cubic-yard Euclid lorry. I have a basic wage of £18 per week, and my take-home pay is less than £17 for a wife and four children. My earnings are so low that I qualify for family supplement which includes free milk, school milk for my children, and welfare foods for the baby. … There are people working at Baglan Bay with exactly the same lorries earning anything from £30 to £35 per week.

But my abiding memory of 1972 is the power cuts, particularly looking across the West London night sky at six o'clock in the evening, lights in the high-rise flats extinguished to the south, and simultaneously re-lit to the north: the benign power of the miners, which also accidentally re-kindled a mass market in candles and invented 'boil-in-the-bag' food for pubs and restaurants.

For my father and mother it was sweet revenge for the indignity and long nightmare of 1926 and its bitter aftermath. Two years later, in 1974, the miners inadvertently brought down the Conservative Government because Prime Minister Edward Heath mistakenly asked the fateful question, 'Who runs the country?' No doubt my father and the other miners' leaders enjoyed their tea (my father didn't drink beer) and sandwiches at No. 10. 1974, he said, was a picnic compared with 1972.

I remember well the new Employment Secretary, Michael Foot, conceding the miners' demands, wearing the South

Wales miners' 1972 badge. Ten years later it was another story. Different times, different leaders, different strategies and very different governments. It was revenge of another kind. Suffice to say, for me, London played an even bigger part in the miners' struggle, and not unlike the solidarity of 1926. By then I was teaching and organising day release and evening classes for University College Swansea, mainly in Valley communities. I became chair of the Neath, Dulais and Swansea Valley Miners' Support Group and eventually I chaired the Wales Congress in Support of Mining Communities. 1984–85 had many echoes of 1926, not least because both were lengthy disputes, and not least because we looked to London for both solidarity and a resolution of the dispute – and also, unlike 1972 and 1974, disunity was a defining factor of the struggle.

As in 1926, the best organised and most politically conscious coalfield was South Wales. By early summer it was picketing power stations, ports and steelworkers across two-thirds of the landmass of Britain. This was deemed illegal, and the courts sequestrated the South Wales NUM funds. To sustain the strike, fundraising for food distribution was essential. Arthur Scargill allegedly divided up the world: he had given his favourite coalfields, Yorkshire and Kent, the whole of North America and also London. South Wales was given Ireland! We decided in the Neath, Dulais and Swansea Valley Miners' Support Group – and we were later followed by other groups – to go into London, under the radar. We avoided union head offices and contacted local branches, often using our London Welsh connections. My cousin David Henry Williams was a reader in *The Times* in Fleet Street. He was also secretary of London Welsh RFC. He gave us his contacts there and elsewhere so that SOGAT and NGA chapels adopted whole villages, particularly at Christmas time. Our first London donations came from ethnic minority communities, led by black groups in Broadwater Farm and Greek and Turkish Cypriot groups. Areas like Islington raised over £100,000, according to Jeremy Corbyn MP, mainly from payroll deductions. Most of it went to South Wales. A young gay man from Nantgarw started a collection – he was living in London for more 'space', as he called it. Ali Thomas, a striking Blaenant miner, later leader of Neath Port Talbot County Borough Council, and David Donovan, later a BECTU union official, were sent up to receive a cheque at a gay pub in London. The result was the creation of the London Gays and Lesbian Support the Miners' Group and phenomenally successful fundraising concerts by Jimmy Somerville and the Communards, and later the Flying Pickets, Billy Bragg, Elvis Costello and a band called The Men They Couldn't Hang. This broadening of the industrial struggle into a community and cultural struggle led to the creation of the South Wales Striking Miners' Choir which sang frequently in London – and, of course, in Ireland. Even today there are still thank you tours to Ireland!

A key feature of the solidarity in London was the role of women, who through women's groups, trade union groups like Brent NALGO, peace groups like CND, and the gays and lesbians, were the main advocates of the miners' cause. The outstanding speaker in these meetings and rallies was Sian James, from our women's support group, who spoke at the first London Gay Pride March, with the Blaenant NUM banner in pride of place at the head of the march. Her husband, Martin, was a striking Abernant miner. We even launched a London Congress in Support of the Miners, in County Hall, with Sian, myself, Ken Livingstone and Merthyr's Illtyd Harrington, the best Mayor London never had, as speakers.

Towards the end of the strike, I was asked to give the funeral oration at Hendon Crematorium for the retired miners' leader Will Paynter, who had died just before Christmas. At the end of the oration I made reference to his dislike of the 'cult of personality'. These were my words:

> … as one young south Wales miner said the day he died, 'Bill Paynter was not a god and he certainly didn't see himself as one'. As we all know, he was to the last a very humble, self-effacing man.

Kim Howells said after I finished, 'That was a great attack on Scargill!' There was nothing further from my mind.

I will end not with a strike at all but with two enduring cultural statements which signify the permanence of the relationship between the miners and London, a kind of love affair which we should all celebrate.

The Festival of Britain in 1951 was indeed a celebration of peacetime Britain. For me it was a twin celebration of a new kind of civilisation which brought coal into public ownership, an industry managed by the NCB on behalf of the people, and its greatest enduring legacy, the National Health Service, whose architect was a South Wales miner, Aneurin Bevan. The Festival of Britain's enduring legacy is, of course, the Royal Festival Hall at the heart of London's then new centre of the arts on the South Bank. It was best symbolised by the artist Josef Herman, the Polish refugee, who in living amongst the miners of Ystradgynlais, was commissioned by the Festival Committee to paint the mural, *Miners*, to represent the new Britain which the miners had sacrificed so much to create.

I have tried tonight to relate, recall, explain the many-layered benign relationships between the miners and London – indeed the affections of one another.

The poet Idris Davies should have the last word. The one-time miner was a school teacher. His poem 'Marx and Heine and Dowlais' says it all about our enduring mostly happy relationships which opens with the lines:

I used to go to St John's Wood
On Saturday evenings in summer
To look on London behind the dusty garden trees,
And argue pleasantly and bitterly
About Marx and Heine, the iron brain and the laughing sword;
And the ghosts of Keats would sit in a corner …

19

David Carpanini: 1969, 'The Cape' and the Last Smiling Shift*

D AVID CARPANINI AND I have much in common: most obviously, we were both born in 1946 into the South Wales Valleys and we enthusiastically acknowledge that these distinctive community roots shaped our values and our vision.

We also come from the tops of our valleys, which I have half jokingly said gave us a particularly far-sighted vision. I made this remark when I opened David's exhibition in Swansea's Attic Gallery nearly a decade ago. My village of Onllwyn in the Dulais Valley and his village of Abergwynfi in the Afan Valley within my constituency of Aberavon have the same vantage point as Blaenllechau in the Rhondda Fach, looking down our respective valleys as we do.

By the same token, David has given us clarity of vision from the personal vantage point of our formative post-war years, which I believe is unique in that everyone in the Valleys can understand clearly what they see and can connect to his work. He has captured that moment in time in our early lives.

★ Text of a lecture to open the exhibition *David Carpanini, Painter, Printmaker and his world: A retrospective, 1964–2014* at Leamington Spa Art Gallery and Museum, 24 January 2014.

And if David tries to tell you that none of the characters in his work resemble anyone, they should speak to everyone from Abergwynfi and Blaengwynfi who will all agree with my neighbour Diane – originally from Blaengwynfi – who said earlier this month, 'there's Dai Smout and that's Jersey Road', in his painting entitled *I remember well how we thought we were so grown up*. But they are all wrong; I know because David told me so.

One academic, Graham Humphrys, from David's neighbouring Llynfi Valley, has written of the time and the place in this way:

> ln 1945, the traditional economic inheritance still dominated the region. South Wales was still basically a nineteenth-century place in a twentieth-century world. The coal and steel industries reigned supreme, the transport system was organised to suit their needs and little else, the region's social capital such as housing had been little added to since the Edwardian period. It was not just that the overall industrial structure had seen little change. Individual industries still wore their nineteenth-century forms. Steel sheets were still being hand-dipped in molten tin to make tin-plate in small scattered works. Colliers still picked coal by hand from two-foot seams and afterwards went home to wash in a tin bath in front of the fire. Many of the hospitals were condemned, and in many places things like bread, milk and coal were still being delivered by horse and cart. [And I can add in my valley ice cream was delivered by horse and cart.]

David has, of course, characterised all this in a very personal way. He has said:

> I believe that man has a special bond with that part of the earth which nourishes his boyhood and it is in the Valleys and the former mining communities of South Wales, scarred by industrialisation but home for a resolute people, that I have found the trigger for my imagination.

Imagination and indeed creativity are the key words then, not nostalgia. That time of 1945 shaped a South Wales which in turn re-shaped Britain and the world. This was the South Wales which produced Aneurin Bevan and in turn our National Health Service. It was the South Wales of Richard Burton on the world's stage and screen and the greatest voice in the English language. And it was the South Wales Valleys of such great writers as Menna Gallie, Gwyn Thomas and Elaine Morgan, all sons and daughters of miners who remembered the best of a bad world and creatively asked why that sense of community could not inhabit our post-industrial world when we explore, as David suggests, 'aspects of the human condition'.

Valleys people see themselves as different. Peculiarly, today, by birth, they are the most Welsh in Wales. And yet equally peculiarly, by origin, our antecedents are the most diverse. My father said we were French Huguenots.

My friend Dai Smith, in his inimitable way, put it this way in writing about the work of the Rhondda artist Ernest Zobole:

> There has never been anything remotely normal about the sudden peopling of the landscape of the central valleys of South Wales.

I suppose wc all see ourselves as different and we celebrate our diversity and our creativity: the Jewish refugee and painter Josef Herman (Joe Bach), the Abercraf and Dowlais Spaniards and the Italians in virtually every community, undoubtedly end up becoming the most creative amongst us. Aberdare's Gabriel Servini, an audacious outside-half, Cwm's outrageously funny Victor Spinetti and Abercraf's linguist Gregorio Esteban, who taught Spanish through the medium of Welsh, were all David Carpanini's illustrious Valleys forerunners.

No Valleys mining community in 1946 was a proper Valleys community unless it had its Italian café. My father insisted that the exact halfway point between Onllwyn and Cardiff was Abercynon's Bracci's because he enjoyed once again Andrew Carpanini's excellent coffee and excellent conversation. David tells me that Andrew was his uncle. And, of course, in my constituency of Aberavon, the 'Parliament of Skewen' is Cresci's, which has the best coffee, the best ham sandwiches and the best political discussions and gossip for miles around.

It could be argued that the formative decade for David was not the late 1940s of his childhood, full of hope as it was, but the 1960s of his youth, full of the anguish and despair of pit closures. After all, his valley was the first of the South Wales Valleys to lose all its pits.

The lonely, often seemingly vulnerable, figures are those of his teenage years. Down the valley from his village, the Duffryn Rhondda colliery closed at the very time of the Aberfan disaster in the autumn of 1966; the floods in Western Europe at that time engulfed both Aberfan and Florence.

David's paintings and drawings of the late 1960s find more than an echo in the poetry of Bryn Griffiths. Lines from 'The Death of Duffryn Rhondda' provide a haunting symmetry which begins in this way:

> The colliery has closed this day, bringing to a bleak end the long years in the lamp-starred darkness, and the miners now wander blindly into another darkness of despair.

That sensitivity continues into succeeding decades where isolation is as ever imbued with empathy and solidarity. Looking at David's paintings of the dramatic years of the mid-1980s, especially his *The nameless began with no end* (1984) and *On Strike* (1985), reminds me of the lively yet despairing, almost nihilistic discussions in the adult evening classes I had in Blaengwynfi during that period. One member of that class, Barbara Walters of Glyncorrwg, a marvellous short-story writer, could well have been describing the atmosphere conjured up by David in those difficult times:

> On the dole, it's a lonely place … you don't talk about being poor if you are poor because you've got so much pride … I was going up the old pit for a walk the other day and this woman was coming down with an empty flask. She said, 'I've just been taking him a cup of tea.' I thought, 'What the hell has she been taking him a cup of tea for?' It then occurred to me that he was picking coal and had been for four years. I forgot the woman's husband – and I'm supposed to be sensitive to people – she'd been taking him a flask of tea. And she said, 'It's a lonely place up there.

I will end on a very personal note for both of us. I once asked David to explain a large charcoal drawing of three young men. 'Why are they smiling and why do they look alike?' I said. He replied, 'They are all brothers and it's their last shift underground, that's why they are smiling.' I said, 'Then it must be September 1969.' He looked more than slightly surprised, and I think he said, 'How do you know that?' I said it was the date of the closure of Afan Ocean Colliery in David's village, known as 'the Cape' because of its apparent remoteness. It was a young workforce and the National Coal Board wanted them transferred to the Llynfi Valley because of a shortage of miners. But none went. They preferred to go down the valley to better, cleaner, safer jobs at Ford in Swansea, BP in Baglan Bay and the steelworks in Port Talbot.

But this was a wistful smile, a smile almost of pathos. It was as if they sensed the imminent loss of pit and community solidarity.

The occasion was of historic significance. It was a defining moment. A threatened coalfield-wide strike to support the Cape failed, but within six weeks there was a strike in support of poorly paid disabled surface workers. That strike was called by some the

'October Revolution', and began the journey to the successful strikes of 1972 and 1974 over what now has a very contemporary resonance, a 'Living Wage'! Those three young miners did have something to smile about, and will continue to smile as long as David Carpanini continues to paint and draw aspects of the human condition.

But revealingly, those smiles appear so often in David's work. Equally revealing, his characters are always tidily, smartly dressed. I interpret in those smiles and tidy appearance perhaps not resistance, but certainly individual and collective resilience, indeed a strong sense of dignity. And I suppose that is what we celebrate today, fifty years of David Carpanini, reminding us of our common humanity.

I feel it is a privilege to be with you today, especially to have David do me the honour of inviting me here as his real Member of Parliament.

And now, David, on to the next fifty years!

20

Democratic Devolution – An Opportunity not a Problem for Human Rights*

WE MEET TODAY THIRTY years on from one of the great human rights struggles which dramatically shaped my own political outlook and that of my generation: the miners' strike of 1984–85. Its manifestation in Wales, despite the hardship, gave rise, it is my belief, to the National Assembly for Wales which has become a champion of the cause of equality and human rights.

At the outset, I should say that I am someone who has supported the cause of democratic devolution since the 1970s and I continue to do so today. As chair now of the UK Parliament's Joint Committee on Human Rights I see our current enquiry into devolution and human rights as an opportunity to survey the impact of the Human Rights Act and the Equality Act – and the international human rights treaties to which the UK has signed up – on the devolved parts of the UK. It is also an opportunity to learn how devolved administrations and parliaments can learn from each other and indeed teach some lessons to the centre – to Whitehall and the mother of Parliaments at Westminster.

---

* Text of speech to the Equality and Human Rights Commission, Cardiff, 10 March 2014.

Let me give you two examples from my own parliamentary experience.

Firstly, in taking through my Private Members' Bill which became the Carers (Equal Opportunities) Act in 2004, I was very focused on the unevenness of human rights and equal opportunities across the UK. I referred to it at the time as a Bill made in Wales from the lived experiences of my constituents who were carers. It was an England and Wales Bill or, as I characterised it, a Wales and England Bill. It was based in part on advances already in place, thanks to the devolved administrations in Northern Ireland and Scotland. Thanks also to the existence of the devolved Welsh Government and my good working relationship with the then Health Minister Jane Hutt, I was always able to ask the UK Carers' Minister Steve Ladyman, when there was a stalling point in the Bill's progress, 'What does the Welsh Health Minister think?', knowing, of course, that Jane agreed with me on all important matters in relation to the Bill!

And then, of course, there was the creation of the pioneering and indeed powerful Welsh Children's Commissioner. When the UK (or rather England) belatedly created a Children's Commissioner, the Welsh Affairs Committee which I then chaired was able to challenge the Children's Minister for England, Margaret Hodge, and ask her why the English Commissioner had fewer and weaker powers than in Wales, and to say to her that weaker powers in England might undermine the stronger Welsh position.

I see these contradictions not as stumbling blocks but as building blocks for equality and human rights. Nevertheless, these contradictions should not now persist into the new more strongly devolved quasi-federal era.

It is in that spirit that I am here today as an enthusiastic democratic devolutionist, wishing to enhance the cause of human rights and equality in the UK in the spirit of Eleanor

Roosevelt who, in her speech before the UN General Assembly in December 1948 on the adoption of the Universal Declaration of Human Rights, said:

> We stand today at the threshold of a great event both in the life of the United Nations and in the life of mankind. This declaration may well become the international Magna Carta for all men everywhere. We hope its proclamation by the General Assembly will be an event comparable to the proclamation in 1789 [the French Declaration of the Rights of Citizens], the adoption of the Bill of Rights by the people of the US, and the adoption of comparable declarations at different times in other countries.

But more significant for us today are Eleanor Roosevelt's other words a decade later in 1958, which are rooted in the lived experiences of families, communities and workplaces:

> Where, after all, do universal human rights begin? In small places, close to home – so close and so small that they cannot be seen on any maps of the world. Yet they are the world of the individual person; the neighbourhood he lives in; the school or college he attends; the factory, farm, or office where he works. Such are the places where every man, woman, and child seeks equal justice, equal opportunity, equal dignity without discrimination. Unless these rights have meaning there, they have little meaning anywhere. Without concerted citizen action to uphold them close to home, we shall look in vain for progress in the larger world.

For me it is that clarity of purpose, rooted in people's daily lives, which inspires us all. In our meeting last week with the chair of this Commission, Baroness O'Neill, I was greatly encouraged by the outline she and her colleagues gave of where you as a Commission are going, with such a strong focus on protecting the most vulnerable and marginalised, realising the rights of people with disabilities, and fairer workplaces.

But I think, given why we are all here today, I must say something about my Committee's inquiry into devolution and human rights. The idea of this inquiry was circulating in and around our work for a while, but we formally agreed before Christmas to dedicate some of our time in 2014 and early 2015 to assess to what extent the current devolutionary settlements (in so far as they are static, and events in Scotland later in the year may prove how dynamic they are!) have assisted, or have held back, the protection and promotion of human rights. My Committee will be calling for written evidence later in the year, taking some oral evidence, and then reporting in 2015 before the General Election. We hope that the report we issue will be of use to the new Parliament and the new Government – and to other key institutions such as yourself.

My Committee is also clear from its work how the whole issue of local government could be wrapped up under this title of devolution. We understand how the problem of transmitting responsibility for human rights from central government to local government is a great challenge – something, Baroness O'Neill, you stressed to the Committee when we spoke about devolution at your pre-appointment hearing eighteen months ago. However, such an inquiry is perhaps for another Parliament, and another JCHR!

Now, I was in Belfast with members of my Committee on Thursday of last week. It was the first in a series of three visits we will be making in connection with this inquiry – we intend to visit Edinburgh in May or June and then we will come here to Cardiff, we hope, in October. It was a useful visit. We managed to cover a number of significant issues – women's rights, children's rights, and, of course, the issue of transitional justice and dealing with the past – and we tried to look at all of these things from the perspective of devolution, to see how such a wide range of matters was being dealt with in Northern Ireland *by the people of Northern Ireland*.

We also, of course, explored how the Executive there – principally the Office of First Minister/deputy First Minister – and the Assembly dealt with human rights issues in policy development, in reporting to international bodies, in scrutinising policy and legislation. I won't go into detail here – not least because Northern Ireland, of course, falls outside your own remit – but clearly the unusual political context there still dominates so much of what goes on, that some important human rights activity is frustrated and thwarted, although some other areas clearly flourish.

But two general themes arose during our discussions time and time again, whether it was with regard to justice and policing, violence against women and girls, children's wider participation in civil society – or even some things as potentially dry as the scrutiny of Bills and the assumption of obligations under international human rights treaties. Those two things were communication and accountability.

Devolution ought to enhance both communication and accountability. The distance from central Government in Whitehall, or from the Westminster Parliament, to a retired couple on benefits in Swansea, or to a migrant family in Glasgow, or to a group of unemployed teenagers in Belfast, can for all practical purposes be immense. Remote government can be inaccessible, effectively silent and invisible – and thus unaccountable and irrelevant. Bringing governments and parliaments – and other institutions – closer to the people should only enhance communication. And with easier communication comes greater accountability – after all, unless a message is intelligible, no-one can properly be held to account for its content.

And what can we say of the accountability of the devolved government of London? What are the complex questions there particularly on the continually vexed accountability of policing?

I had the privilege of attending the launch of the Welsh

Government's Strategy for Independent Living in September 2012, which showed how devolution can lead to strides forward in human rights provision in at least one area of the United Kingdom. This, I believe, was the fruit of good communication with disabled people in Wales who gave evidence to us – and full accountability to them – and the fruit of full participation by the disabled community in Wales in political discourse.

But there is a flip-side to this. Unless there is clarity in communication about responsibility for human rights, unless every link in the chain of devolution communicates clearly and cooperatively in both directions, the chance of unaccountability (and of confusion) remains – and with confusion can come misunderstanding, and with misunderstanding distrust. I can recall the words of Professor O'Flaherty, then chair of the Northern Ireland Human Rights Commission, in an evidence session before my Committee at the end of 2011:

> On the one hand, devolution can bring human rights much closer to the rights holders … On the other hand … [there can be] … great difficulty in translating the … human rights obligation from London to the devolved capital … to encourage the political leaders at that level that they carry with them the responsibility of the state to deliver not just on the European Convention but also on the array of other treaties.

The more links there are in the chain, the easier it can be for some to believe or assume that others will take the strain, that responsibility for areas of human rights strategy, or policy, or promotion and protection, lie elsewhere. Even when there is goodwill on all sides, new arrangements and the new relationship they establish require time to explore, to navigate and properly to understand. I note that the Silk Commission only last week recommended changes to the devolutionary settlement here which will – if accepted – usher in further changes which will need bedding down until accountability and communication become clear.

Some of these difficulties in accountability and communication are inevitable, especially when devolution is still new, and devolved institutions are coming to terms with their relationship to central government and to other bodies. The confusion that abounded in some policy areas in Westminster following devolution, as to what sort of questions could be tabled by MPs to the NIO, the Scotland Office or even to the Wales Office, was considerable. The devolution Acts set down in writing areas of the 'new constitution' of the UK for the first time, but with the rest still famously unwritten it was like having a jigsaw puzzle where half of the pieces were still largely blank. The complete picture was still difficult to grasp.

Some difficulties are also a function of complexity – and the devolution settlement in Northern Ireland is the most complex of the three in the UK. Complexity can still bedevil human rights policy today, whether it is areas where children's rights overlap areas of immigration policy – as we found out in our inquiry into migrant children – or where matters relating to housing and benefits have enormous potential implications for issues connected with justice and community relations, which may in turn have consequences for policing – as the discussions in Northern Ireland in 2012 over the Welfare Reform Bill made clear. You yourselves will be aware of the importance of good relationships, good communication and – where necessary – memoranda of understanding between you and central institutions and with other devolved bodies, so you can know exactly where the buck stops, where responsibilities lie, who will do what and how you will take your work forward cooperatively with greatest effect.

But some challenges are down to what I might politely call idleness and mischief. In so far as devolution breeds bureaucracies, idleness can be a greater menace than before. And political failure in just one area of the chain will break it, no matter how many links there are. The failure of the Northern Ireland Executive to input important reports to UN bodies with regard to two – possibly three – international human rights treaties wasn't a matter of confusion or of idleness (the officials did all that they could and seem to have done it well) but of failure of political will to do what ought to have been done. When this failure – or neutralisation – of political will, clear in Northern Ireland, can hold up the proper protection and promotion of human rights, and when the will (or means) of the Government in Whitehall to remedy that failure is lacking, then it comes down (as always it must) to the people. As Bob Collins of the Equality Commission for Northern Ireland pointed out to us in oral evidence in December 2011, this is one conundrum of devolution: what should happen when 'a local administration can operate at a slower pace than the nation as a whole'?

I haven't made much reference to political will – this is because this has to be a given for there to be real progress in human rights. Devolution ought to allow for that political will to develop and be strengthened to reflect what people want their representatives, their government, to do. Of course, the issue of political will is one area of the human rights arena in Northern Ireland where the principal difficulties lie, especially with regard to transitional justice. But some areas of what was once a complete impasse have broken down – in the area of policing much has been done (although much remains to be done). So where there's a will there *is* a way. And the more accountable a parliament and a government are to their people, and the more those people can communicate what they want to those who lead in their society, then the greater ought be the political will of those leaders to act.

And so we come back to the quotation from Eleanor Roosevelt that I used earlier in this speech – with human rights beginning in 'small places, close to home'. The great hope for progressive realisation of all our rights rests with the people – that is, with us. And that is surely one of the greatest lessons that devolution can teach us.

21

The Hope for a
Compassionate Country[*]

Gᴀ I ᴇsᴛʏɴ, ғᴇʟ cadeirydd Byw Nawr, groeso cynnes i chi i gyd i gynhadledd gyntaf Byw Nawr. Mae'n addas iawn i ni gwrdd yma yng Nghaerdydd, ein prifddinas.

As chair of Byw Nawr/Live Now, I am delighted to welcome you to our first conference. It is a particular pleasure to have with us our Health Secretary, Vaughan Gething: he and his predecessor Professor Mark Drakeford have been very supportive of our End of Life Care Coalition in Wales. And I should also add that our Deputy Health Secretary Rebecca Evans has been especially encouraging of the vision of a 'compassionate country'.

I think we all share the common objectives of striving to achieve a full and dignified end of life for all our citizens, and this is a particularly significant aspiration when we are supporting the most vulnerable in our society.

I should perhaps explain my own personal and indeed political commitment to our common goal, for I do believe that the 'personal is the political'. My wife Mair and I have been members of the Down's Syndrome Association since September 1980

---

[*] Text of a speech at the first Byw Nawr Ministerial Conference, Cardiff, 11 May 2017.

when our late son Sam was born with Down's syndrome as well as a serious heart condition. In a short time we were made aware that this was apparently inoperable, that he would have periodic health problems that would worsen in his adolescence. He died aged 16 in 1997 having lived a full and happy life, educated in mainstream bilingual schools.

When I entered Parliament in 2001 as the Member of Parliament for Aberavon, I made a commitment in my Maiden Speech to work for and with people with disabilities and their carers. I have to acknowledge that in sponsoring my Carers (Equal Opportunities) Act in 2004, chairing the all-party carers' and Down's syndrome groups as well as the Joint Committee on Human Rights, the question of end of life care was only beginning to emerge as a critical policy area – certainly in my own mind – even though as parents we had direct experience of it.

In this respect, I have to acknowledge the work of my friends – significantly, all women – Baroness Ilora Finlay on Palliative Care, Baroness Jane Campbell on Independent Living and Councillor Sara Pickard of Mencap Cymru on Health Passports for people with Down's syndrome. Of course, in the case of Jane and Sara, their work was not exclusively on end of life care. All three have been outstanding in raising important health and caring issues in complementary ways, locally, nationally and internationally.

I agreed to become chair of Byw Nawr on one condition. In embracing the philosophy of a glass half full, I suggested that the name of the network in Wales should be a positive one and reflect more a zest for life rather than an acceptance of death. After all, as we approach the end of our lives we are still living and we aspire to achieve full and dignified lives to the very end, and that surely is more about life than it is about death.

When Baroness Ilora Finlay, chair of the National Council for Palliative Care, gave the Annual Aneurin Bevan Lecture in 2016, she quoted the words of the late Dame Cicely Saunders, pioneer of the hospice movement and palliative care in modern medicine. Dame Cicely said:

> You matter because you are you, and you matter to the last moment of your life. We will do all we can, not only to help you die peacefully but also *to live until you die* [my emphasis].

Her words should be our guiding inspiration and that is why my contribution today is entitled 'the hope for a compassionate country'.

I would like to talk to you about what Byw Nawr has done as a network in Wales in little over two and a half years, and how this has led us towards a campaign for a compassionate country. Byw Nawr is a partnership, and we like to describe it also as a broad and inclusive community, committed to help generate a *Big Conversation* in Wales about how we can live well, yet make preparations in advance for end of life.

The partnership supports the Welsh Government's End of Life Care Delivery Plan by promoting 'a healthy realistic approach to dying, adopting healthy lifestyles while being informed and supported to make arrangements in advance for the end of life'.

Our partnership steering group includes a wide range of organisations from Marie Curie and Macmillan to the Law Society, Age Cymru and Carers Wales, along with what we call 'user representation', people who have direct personal experience of end of life care, often as family members. We have held events at a variety of locations – at the National Eisteddfod, the Hay Festival (with the OU in Wales, and Marie Curie this year) and at the Senedd when many AMs pledged to support our work.

Many of us are enthusiastic supporters of the social model described as *compassionate communities*, as proposed by Professor Allan Kellehear of the University of Bradford, who recently gave a lecture in Cardiff sponsored by Marie Curie and Lord Dafydd

Elis-Thomas AM. I pay tribute to Simon Jones of Marie Curie for initiating the discussion in Wales on this. As chair of Byw Nawr I believe we can take this idea forward in Wales, using the Welsh Government's Wellbeing and Future Generations Act alongside Public Health Wales to develop a civic or community approach. This has already been achieved in cities as far afield as Seville, Londonderry/Derry and Birmingham, and communities and regions as different as Frome and Inverclyde.

Professor Kellehear told us that the most successful health interventions worldwide are essentially civic, as with clean water; so too then with end of life care, with befriending strategies between young and old. The compassionate cities charter is a good framework, with a focus on our schools, our workplaces, our churches and temples, even our museums and galleries.

I would like to pay tribute to my local authority, Neath Port Talbot County Borough Council, in being the first local authority in Wales to adopt a policy strategy of being a compassionate employer, a strategy encouraged by both the Wales TUC and the Wales CBI. Next year is the seventieth anniversary of the NHS. What better way of celebrating this than by launching *Compassionate Cymru* – in Tredegar, with the Aneurin Bevan Health Board? After all, this is where it all began: Wales' gift to the world. And Wales would be the first compassionate country in the world. How appropriate.

I will end on that positive note, and by expressing the hope that our compassionate Cymru, dedicated not so much to full and dignified deaths, rather as I would prefer to put it, to full and dignified lives, to the very end.

Postscript

On 1 July 2018 the Welsh Cabinet Secretary for Health, Vaughan Gething, announced that it was his ambition for Wales to become the first 'Compassionate Country'.

Also from Y Lolfa:

ABERFAN

A Story of Survival, Love and Community
in One of Britain's Worst Disasters

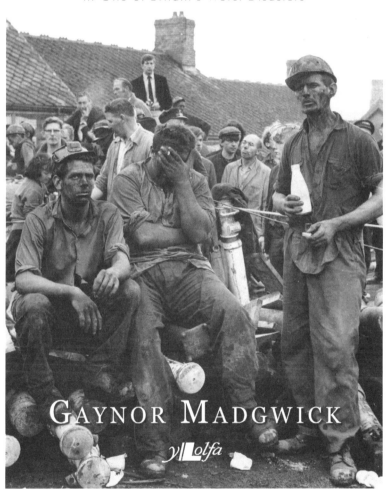

GAYNOR MADGWICK

yLolfa

£9.99

Sam Adams

Where the
Stream Ran Red
Memories and Histories
of a Welsh Mining Valley

£9.99

John Davies

"One of the most influential
Welshmen of our era."
– **Richard Wyn Jones**

y Lolfa

A Life in History

£9.99

LIFE IN THE COAL HOUSE

THE GRIFFITHS FAMILY

WITH ALUN GIBBARD

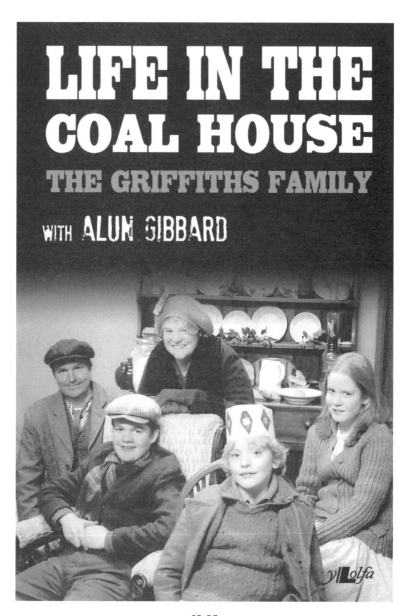

£3.95

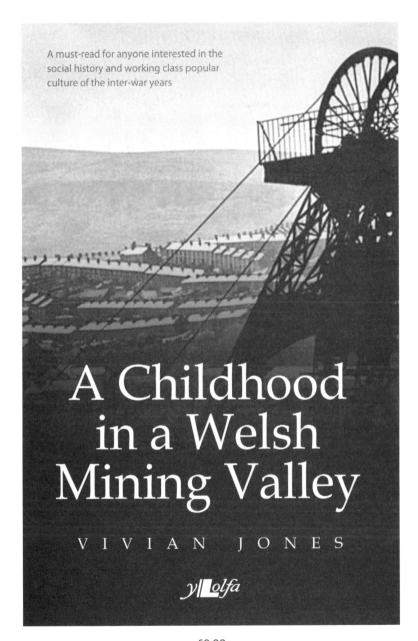

A must-read for anyone interested in the social history and working class popular culture of the inter-war years

A Childhood in a Welsh Mining Valley

VIVIAN JONES

y Lolfa

£9.99

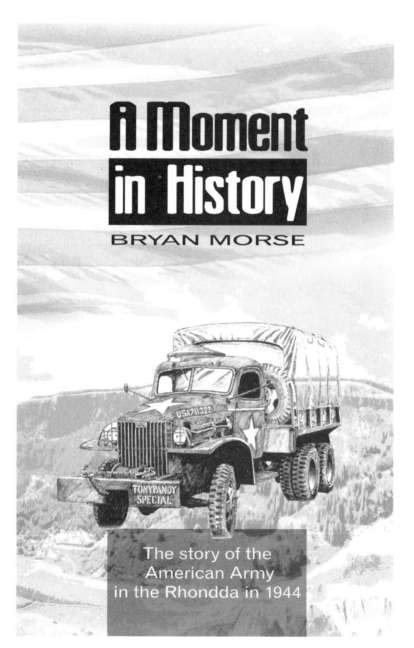

A Moment in History

in History

BRYAN MORSE

The story of the
American Army
in the Rhondda in 1944

£9.95